Conservative Options Trading

Conservative Options Trading

Hedging Strategies, Cash Cows, and Loss Recovery

Michael C. Thomsett

BEP BUSINESS EXPERT PRESS

Conservative Options Trading: Hedging Strategies, Cash Cows, and Loss Recovery

Copyright © Business Expert Press, LLC, 2020.

Cover image licensed by Ingram Image, StockPhotoSecrets.com

First published in 2020 by
Business Expert Press, LLC
222 East 46th Street, New York, NY 10017
www.businessexpertpress.com

ISBN-13: 978-1-95152-712-9 (paperback)
ISBN-13: 978-1-95152-713-6 (e-book)

Business Expert Press Finance and Financial Management Collection

Collection ISSN: 2331-0049 (print)
Collection ISSN: 2331-0057 (electronic)

Cover and interior design by Exeter Premedia Services Private Ltd., Chennai, India

First edition: 2020

10 9 8 7 6 5 4 3 2 1

Printed in the United States of America.

Abstract

The world of options is considered high risk by many. At its original options trading in the modern era began in the early 1970s when the first listed calls were offered on a short list of companies; a few years later, put trading was added.

Since this time, options trading has become available on most companies on the large public exchanges. However, the high-risk reputation of options has persisted through the years, even as dozens of new and often conservative strategies have been introduced. Today, the best use of options is not to speculate on price movement, but to hedge market risk in equity portfolios. Many strategies can combine hedging with income, establishing advantageous circumstances for risk-averse traders. It is possible to apply several strategies to reduce risk and, in some instances, to eliminate market risk completely.

This book examines the many ways this can be accomplished, based on options for three highly rated companies. These are qualified as a first step by exceptionally attractive fundamental attributes and trends: Higher than average dividend yield with dividend increases over at least 10 years; a range of moderate price/earnings ratios each year; growing revenue, earnings, and net return; and level or declining long-term debt as a percentage of total capitalization.

Keywords

Bollinger bands; chart analysis; conservative; portfolio; volatility; downside risk; exercise; extrinsic value; intrinsic value; time value; implied volatility; spread; straddle; insurance put; covered call; LEAPS options; leverage; momentum; contingent purchase; contingent sale; speculation; strike price; expiration; underlying security; tax rules; rescue strategies; risk; long; short

Contents

Introduction

The Elusive Goal: Low Risk and High Yield

The elusive goal for every trader is to achieve the combination of low risk and high yield. Is this ever possible?

The market invariably brings you both good news and bad news. The bad news: Markets are volatile and risky, and any capital placed at risk could result in losses, at times catastrophic losses. The good news: These market risks can be hedged effectively using *conservative* options strategies.

Coupling the words "conservative" and "options" may seem surprising, since the long-standing reputation of the options market has been exotic, high risk, and inappropriate for many if not most investors, both institutional and retail.

This does not have to be the case.

The options market is becoming increasingly recognized as much more than a form of pure speculation. Today, growing numbers of investors are recognizing that options are most effective as tools for managing a portfolio, reducing and eliminating its risks through hedging strategies, and improving profits.

This book demonstrates how a conservative portfolio can be made safer and more secure, while increasing income. This is accomplished through the combination of equity positions with specific and conservative options strategies. The intention is not merely to augment net profits but to protect the profitability of the equity side of the portfolio as well. This idea is dramatic in the positive effect it has on an institutional portfolio.

The problem every investor and trader faces is twofold: First and foremost, investment decisions must be conservative enough to protect against losses. It means that many opportunities must be passed up because the risks are perceived as too great. Second, the goal must be to match and beat inflation and taxes, the double impact that demands seeking higher returns.

How can you seek higher returns in this portfolio, while continuing to observe the essential demand for conservative strategic management?

Many market insiders and experts are pessimists on this question. They point out that your chance is only through broad diversification of risk, and complex asset allocation as management tools. Both ideas present profound problems for every portfolio. Broad diversification means trying to attain the "vanilla" medium return of the market. A majority of mutual funds, for example, are broadly diversified but they underperform the market average. In fact, according to one source, the average actively managed stock mutual fund returns much less than the overall market. In 2017, the returns for the three major indices and for mutual funds were:

Dow Jones Industrial Average	25.08%
S&P 500	21.83%
NASDAQ	29.64%
U.S. *mutual funds*	18.26%[1]

It was not just a one-year dismal report. Making matters worse, even beyond the average outcome, most funds perform beneath the average of the broader market. One study concluded that over 15 years, an average of more than 90 percent of funds reported yields *lower* than the overall market:

% yielding less	
than market average	
All mutual funds	83.74%
Large cap	92.33%
Mid cap	94.81%
Small cap	95.73%
Average	91.65%[2]

Why is this so? The answer is at the crux of the message in this book. Any observer of the mutual fund performance phenomenon would

---

[1] https://investors.com/etfs-and-funds/mutual-funds/mutual-fund-performance-2017/

[2.] http://aei.org/publication/more-evidence-that-its-very-hard-to-beat-the-market-2.over-time-95-of-financial-professionals-cant-do-it/

wonder why the average mutual fund underperforms market averages *and* why most funds perform under market averages.

The three disadvantages mutual funds have over other institutions (e.g., insurance companies, banks, pension plans, and specialized advisory service provides) include overdiversification, fees, and requirements for cash on hand. Mutual funds—notably very large ones—may simply hold positions in too many segments of the market, so that their returns are going to be average at best. Returns are further diminished by fees that mutual funds charge (1.44 percent on average). Finally, funds hold between 3 and 7 percent in cash to meet obligations, and this "dead money" does not earn.

Other institutions that may be less concerned with competition or with performance reporting are not as likely to suffer from this dismal outcome. However, an underlying problem is that every investor, whether an individual or a portfolio manager, must contend with the desire for better returns without higher risks. This is a daunting task; but the options market addresses these concerns and improves chances for meeting both otherwise conflicting goals.

A central theme of this book is to analyze the possibility for matching acceptable risks with better than average yields. Most experts question the idea that risk-averse investors can outperform the market averages. However, this book challenges the conventional wisdom by demonstrating how conservative investors can exploit a narrow band of potential strategies, dramatically increase yields and, at the same time, manage risks within their self-defined risk limitations.

Risk is at the core of all ideas for portfolio management. If a range of strategies contains too many pitfalls, it is not worth pursuing. But a basic premise in this book is that a conservative investor is not necessarily someone who does not want to expand beyond a well-understood and short list of investment possibilities. Being a conservative investor does not necessarily mean that you are unwilling to examine new ideas, expand your portfolio, or take acceptable risks. It just means that you are not interested in speculation or in exposing yourself to the possibilities of high risk. This applies to personal comfort levels or preferences and to internally imposed standards and limits. Many investors attempt to carefully define acceptable risks with the intention of avoiding unacceptable losses. This translates to a complete ban on options trading, and for good reasons.

In the recent past, abuses of derivatives trading created many losses and a troubling question about whether those individuals making portfolio decisions represented the investment policies of the institution. In 2008, many options-based institutional trades resulted in massive losses, including Morgan Stanley[3] ($9.6 billion) and Société Générale[4] ($6.6 billion).

These losses do not include losses in futures or credit default swaps, which in many cases were even larger. Even so, the options market has received the worst press as overly risky, often abused, and far too speculative for conservative investment managers or individual investors. It is true that a lack of experience or awareness of risks most likely leads to large losses. It is not enough for an institution to rely on an individual who has studied options and passed the FINRA Series 4 exam (Registered Options Principal) if that person does not have experience in trading and is not aware of the range of risks in speculative trading practices.

This book offers a realistic definition of "conservative investing" which is a series of polices practiced by those experienced enough to be aware of both yield and risk and who make decisions based on awareness. Conservative investors are not as likely as other investors to be taken by surprise when they lose money in the market. Another aspect of this expanded definition distinguishes between risk profile and the willingness to use creative and alternative strategies. Conservative investors are not close-minded and do not reject exotic instruments like options merely because of their reputation as high risk. Instead, well-informed conservative investors are likely to examine claims about high-yield potential with an open mind. You may be skeptical and, at the same time, willing to listen to the suggestion that the combination is at least possible. A limited number of strategies do, in fact, offer the potential for conservative applications to

---

[3] Howie, H. 2010. "The Return of a Subprime Villain." *The New York Observer,* March 24.

[4] Schwartz, N. 2008. "A Spiral of Losses by a 'Plain Vanilla' Trader." *The New York Times,* January 25.

meet the three goals common to conservative investors: preserving capital, avoiding unacceptable risk, and protecting profits.

This book does not suggest that you must become an expert in a broad range of complex or exotic options strategies. Instead, it proposes a limited number of strategies appropriate for conservative investors. This approach respects the limitations in the conservative risk profile while showing how experienced stock market investors can expand their yield levels significantly, protect existing positions, and come through market down cycles intact.

CHAPTER 1

Setting the Ground Rules

This book explains how conservative investors can employ options strategies to (a) enhance current income without increasing market risks; (b) protect long positions through options used for insurance; and (c) create a form of contingency to survive in volatile market conditions.

The Ground Rules

Since you are a *conservative* investor, the arguments in this book are based on a series of underlying assumptions. These relate to your risk profile and to your investing philosophy. Five underlying assumptions are used in this book:

1. **You will limit options activities to prequalified stocks.** This is a necessary starting point if your portfolio and the stocks you use for options strategies include stocks you believe in as long-term-hold positions, and you consider these stocks as permanent parts of your portfolio (if the fundamentals remain strong). This is an important attribute because it is not conservative to buy stocks solely to use for options strategies. A conservative approach to options must include the premise that your activities will be limited to the strongest possible stocks you can find.

2. **You believe that your stocks will rise in value.** A conservative investor naturally expects stocks to rise in value; otherwise, why keep them? But this obvious point has relevance in the underlying assumptions of this book. Many of the discussions of strategies are premised on a belief that over the long term, the subject stock's market value will rise. However, many options strategies work best when stocks do *not* rise, such as bearish combinations or long put strategies. Covered call writing (a conservative strategy) is most

profitable when stock values remain steady or even fall slightly. This means that you may need to time a strategy to produce profits resulting from short-term stability in prices, hoping for longer-term growth. Many options strategies are designed to take advantage of short-term price volatility. When marketwide volatility affects short-term prices of your stocks, you have an opportunity to pick up discounted shares, take profits (without having to sell stock), or average down your overall basis. Of course, the proposal that you should average down is conservative only if the basic stock selection assumptions remain valid. You will want to employ such a strategy only for stocks in which you have a strong belief as long-term value investments.

3. **You accept the premise that fundamental analysis of stocks is an essential first step in the process of examining option opportunities.** Options have no fundamental attributes. These are intangible contractual instruments, and they have no value on their own; thus, you can only judge the tangible value of stock as a means for selecting appropriate options strategies. Many first-time options traders make the mistake of overlooking this reality. They select options (and stocks) based on the immediate return potential, but they ignore the market risks of the underlying stocks. This violates the conservative tenet that stocks should be chosen for their fundamental strength and growth potential.

4. **In the event of a temporary downward movement in a stock's price, you would be happy to buy more shares.** Some investors may be unwilling to pick up more shares of a stock even when the opportunity to buy discounted shares is presented. In this book, several strategies are introduced proposing that additional shares may be purchased (or exposed to contingent purchase) using options. If this is not the case in a situation, those suggestions should be passed over. You may have a formula for diversification that you use to limit risks in any stocks, for example, so strategies aimed at increasing your holdings in one stock may contradict your portfolio management standards in such an instance. Strategies proposing that you set up situations in which more shares may be picked up work *only* if that suggestion conforms to your overall portfolio plan.

5. **You believe that an adequate number of available stocks meet your criteria.** Some investors become convinced that their short list of stocks is the only list available to them. If they were to sell shares of stock from their portfolio, they would be unable to reinvest profits in equally acceptable stocks. If you do not believe this, you are probably aware that dozens of stocks meet your criteria in terms of price level, price/earnings (PE) ratio, volatility, dividend payment history, and a range of other analytical tests. Accordingly, if a stock is sold from your portfolio, several other stocks that you could and would purchase upon sale of stocks you currently own also conform to your criteria.

This set of rules makes sense whether you trade options or not. The fundamentals can change for any company, so if a "hold" signal changes to "sell," you need to reinvest funds. As a matter of basic portfolio management, every investor needs a secondary list of stocks that would be used to replace sold stocks from the current portfolio. The need for maintaining this list relates to options trading because some strategies result in selling shares of stock. In those cases, you want to reinvest capital in a new issue on your list of qualified stocks.

A Model Portfolio

In the examples used in the following chapters, these five underlying assumptions demonstrate how options work within the conservative framework. These criteria are applied to a model portfolio of three stocks, which are used in various combinations throughout. This helps to tie together the various examples and range of possible outcomes. This model portfolio is by no means a recommendation of stocks you should own. It was selected to include stocks with some common attributes:

- They have increased dividends every year for the past 7 and 10 years (or more) and have reported low volatility in trading.
- Dividend yields are higher than average, between 4.75 and 6.63 percent.

- All these stocks have available both listed options and long-term options (Long-term Equity AnticiPation Security [LEAPS]), enabling you to look at a variety of scenarios for each conservative strategy. Analysis includes a study of options expiring in 1 week, and in 1, 2, 4, and 16 months.
- All reported 10-year PE ranges falling within a moderate range.
- Both revenue and earnings rose during the 10-year period studied.
- Debt to capitalization ratio remained steady or declined over the decade.

Employing a single portfolio throughout the book is helpful in another way. Not every strategy works well for each stock in the model portfolio, so you can walk through the selection process to demonstrate how a strategic decision is made. Although your portfolio may contain several excellent value investments, some strategies simply do not always work in all cases. You can compare the different potentials for strategies across a range of stocks by following the model portfolio throughout the explanations in each chapter.

Table 1.1 summarizes this model portfolio, consisting of AT&T, Southern Co., and Altria and based on valuation at the closings prices of April 25, 2019. These represent three industries: telecommunications, energy, and pharmaceuticals. The portfolio's overall value is estimated at

Table 1.1 Model portfolio

Stock name	Symbol	Closing price *	Shares held	Total value	%
AT&T	T	$30.34	1,400	$ 42,476	33.8%
Southern Co.	SO	52.44	800	41,952	33.4
Altria	MO	51.41	800	41,128	32.8
Total				$125,556	100.0%

*Closing prices as of April 25, 2019.
Source: Charles Schwab & Co.

$125,000, split as equally as possible among the three stocks. This breakdown is summarized in Table 1.1.

These companies were selected based on exceptional fundamentals (dividends, P/E, revenue and earnings, and long-term debt trends). A note concerns the fixed date: This enables comparisons between the three members of the model portfolio on the same date. However, the principles of specific trading strategies may be applied to any company on any date; even though the dates selected are outdated, this does not affect the premise of conservative trade selection and execution.

This portfolio is split equally among the three issues, a modest but effective level of diversification. An individual portfolio is likely to select an entirely different list of stocks, perhaps more than three and perhaps split in a different manner. This is only one example of how a portfolio might be diversified among several value investments (value in this sense defined as having a consistent record of increasing dividends, higher than average dividend yield, medium level of debt ratio, increasing revenues and earnings, and consistent long-term debt management).

This raises a question every investor faces: Is this a "conservative" portfolio? This is a matter of opinion and one that depends on the timing of purchase, long-term goals, and your perception about the fundamentals for each corporation. These stocks provide a cross section of stocks illustrating where strategies work well and where they do not work at all. The definition of a conservative portfolio is (and should be) always evolving based on changes in the market, in a stock's market price and volatility and, of course, in emerging information concerning fundamental strength or weakness of a company.

The values of options for a stock will probably be consistent from one period to the next assuming that the proximity between closing price and option strike price is about the same, and that months to go until expiration are the same as well. Although these relationships vary based on ever-changing perceptions about a company, the data is valid for the purpose of illustrating strategies.

Table 1.2 Option premium, AT&T

AT&T (T)—8 days

Call or put	Strikes	Closing bid	Closing ask
C	29	1.34	1.40
	30	0.49	0.53
	31	0.07	0.09
	32	0.02	0.03
P	29	0.02	0.03
	30	0.16	0.19
	31	0.72	0.76
	32	1.66	1.71

AT&T (T) —29 days

Call or put	Strikes	Closing bid	Closing ask
C	29	1.52	1.58
	30	0.75	0.81
	31	0.25	0.30
	32	0.05	0.08
P	29	0.13	0.18
	30	0.35	0.41
	31	0.87	0.93
	32	1.68	1.74

AT&T (T)—57 days

Call or put	Strikes	Closing bid	Closing ask
C	29	1.71	1.81
	30.50	1.02	1.07
	31	0.50	0.54
	32	0.21	0.23
P	29	0.28	0.32
	30.50	0.57	0.61
	31	1.05	1.10
	32	1.75	1.81

AT&T (T)—85 days

Call or put	Strikes	Closing bid	Closing ask
C	29	1.82	1.90
	30	1.14	1.21
	31	0.64	0.68
	32	0.31	0.35
P	29	0.56	0.60
	30	0.95	0.99
	31	1.49	1.52
	32	2.22	2.29

AT&T (T)—268 days

Call or put	Strikes	Closing bid	Closing ask
C	29	2.31	2.46
	30	1.80	1.88
	31	1.34	1.40
	32	0.85	1.01
P	29	1.60	1.82
	30	2.12	2.21
	31	2.70	2.87
	32	3.30	3.45

Premium values as of April 25, 2019.
Source: Charles Schwab & Co.

The strikes and expirations for AT&T are summarized in Table 1.2 as of the date the study was conducted.

Table 1.3   Option premium, Southern Co.

Southern Co. (SO)—8 days

Call or put	Strikes	Closing bid	Closing ask
C	50	2.03	2.32
	51	1.52	1.79
	52	0.82	1.03
	53	0.29	0.35
	54	0.02	0.12

P	50	0.11	0.16
	51	0.16	0.22
	52	0.34	0.41
	53	0.75	0.89
	54	1.40	1.70

Southern Co. (SO)—29 days

Call or put	Strikes	Closing bid	Closing ask
C	50	2.59	2.95
	51	1.74	2.03
	52	1.00	1.24
	53	0.45	0.61
	54	0.15	0.29
P	50	0.28	0.35
	51	0.46	0.63
	52	0.80	0.99
	53	1.32	1.57
	54	2.03	2.36

Southern Co. (SO)—57 days

Call or put	Strikes	Closing bid	Closing ask
C	50	2.69	2.97
	52.50	0.94	1.01
	55	0.14	0.21
	57.50	0.00	0.17
P	50	0.50	0.55
	52.50	1.26	1.49
	55	2.97	3.35
	57.50	5.10	6.00

Southern Co. (SO)—113 days

Call or put	Strikes	Closing bid	Closing ask
C	50	3.00	3.25
	52.50	1.39	1.54
	55	0.44	0.58

	57.50	0.11	0.21
P	50	0.99	1.11
	52.50	1.95	2.16
	55	3.50	3.90
	57.50	5.60	6.05

Southern Co. (SO)—268 days

Call or put	Strikes	Closing bid	Closing ask
C	50	3.55	3.80
	52.50	2.09	2.32
	55	1.06	1.28
	57.50	0.48	0.59
P	50	1.89	2.08
	52.50	2.94	3.20
	55	4.40	4.70
	57.50	6.30	6.55

Premium values as of April 25, 2019.
Source: Charles Schwab & Co.

The strikes and expirations for Southern Co. are summarized in Table 1.3 as of the date the study was conducted.

The strikes and expirations for Altria are summarized in Table 1.4 as of the date the study was conducted.

Table 1.4 Option premium, Altria
Altria (MO)—8 days

Call or put	Strikes	Closing bid	Closing ask
C	50	1.69	1.82
	51	0.98	1.09
	52.50	0.30	1.36
	53	0.18	0.23
P	50	0.26	0.33
	51	0.53	0.60
	52.50	1.30	1.40
	53	1.67	1.79

Altria (MO)—29 days

Call or put	Strikes	Closing bid	Closing ask
C	50	2.17	2.52
	51	1.54	1.86
	52.50	0.78	1.07
	53	0.60	0.84
P	50	0.68	0.96
	51	0.97	1.30
	52.50	1.66	2.05
	53	2.02	2.57

Altria (MO)—57 days

Call or put	Strikes	Closing bid	Closing ask
C	50	2.53	2.90
	52.50	1.29	1.49
	55	0.51	0.62
P	50	1.36	1.57
	52.50	2.59	2.96
	55	4.40	4.85

Altria (MO)—148 days

Call or put	Strikes	Closing bid	Closing ask
C	50	3.35	3.80
	52.50	2.26	2.51
	55	0.36	0.52
P	50	2.76	2.90
	52.50	3.85	4.40
	55	5.50	5.95

Altria (MO)—268 days

Call or put	Strikes	Closing bid	Closing ask
C	50	4.15	4.60
	52.50	2.91	3.35
	55	2.06	2.40

P	50	3.90	4.35
	52.50	5.15	5.75
	55	6.75	7.35

Premium values as of April 25, 2019.
Source: Charles Schwab & Co.

The wide range of premium values is affected by both time remaining until expiration and the proximity between the strike and the current underlying stock's price. All these values are fixed in time as of the close of business on April 25, 2019, so that comparisons between any of the three are valid.

In coming chapters, dividend yield will also be featured as a prominent part of return calculations. Following is a summary of annual yield for the three companies:

AT&T	6.64%
Southern Co.	4.66
Altria	5.95

Class questions for discussion and/or mini-case studies

Multiple choice

1. The most rational method for selecting stocks to hold in a portfolio is:
   a. Buying shares in the company whose stock has risen the most during the past year.
   b. Looking for the highest volatility in price.
   c. Narrowing the field with a short list of fundamental trends over several years.
   d. Following the financial news and picking stocks the commentators like.
2. The most reliable fundamentals include:
   a. Dividend yield and the trend in long-term debt.
   b. Price changes over the past year.
   c. Price declines, which tend to be followed by price rises.
   d. Percentage of gross assets that have been depreciated.
3. A truly conservative portfolio consists of:
   a. Growth stocks.

  b. Value stocks.

  c. Volatile stocks.

  d. A combination of value and growth.

Exercise for Discussion

Select three stocks of companies with high name recognition (not including the three companies described in this chapter). Study these for a 10-year period and track dividend yield, range of PE ratio, revenue, net profit, and long-term debt capitalization. State your conclusions about whether these companies meet the fundamental criteria for including a company's stock in your portfolio.

CHAPTER 2

Option Basics

The suggestion that options are easy paths to riches does not work for conservative portfolio management. As a conservative investor, you want to know exactly how options might or might not work in your portfolio, and also you want the information to be presented clearly and logically. Since this involves a narrow range of possible strategies—only those appropriate in a conservative portfolio—much of the exotic but high-risk potential of options is avoided.

Even the most experienced investor struggles with terminology and the meaning of key concepts, so this chapter covers the important options basics, including explanations of calls and puts in either long or short positions; how option contracts work; expiration of options; strike prices; and time, extrinsic, and intrinsic values. In discussing the range of possible strategies, the purpose is not to recommend any approach but to explore and review all the possibilities.

The Workings of the Options Contract

The mechanics of expiration, strike price, and time, extrinsic, and intrinsic values affect all decisions related to how you should or should not employ options and how risks increase or decrease as you act to create a strategy.

Option Attributes to Determine Value

Collectively, the attributes of the option contract determine its value. Option contracts refer to 100 shares of stock, meaning that each option contract allows the buyer to control 100 shares of the underlying stock. Every option relates specifically to that one stock and cannot be transferred. The *premium* is the cost (to the buyer) or value (to the seller) of the option. This cost/value is expressed as the value per share, without dollar signs. For example, if an option's current premium is listed as 6, it is worth $600, and if the current premium is listed as 4.75, it is worth $475. Premium is expressed as a single number for round values (like 6) or with two decimals for all others (such as 4.75 or 4.50).

Expiration occurs for all options. The potential profit period for the option speculator is the flip side of the advantage the short seller enjoys. Just as a short seller of stock sells and has an open position, the short seller sells the option. The short option position can be closed in one of three ways. First, it may expire worthless, in which case the entire premium received by the seller is profit. Second, it may be closed by buying to close at any time, with the difference between the initial sales price and final purchase price representing profit or loss. Third, it may be exercised by the buyer, and the short seller will then be obligated to complete the exercise transaction. When a call is exercised, the seller is required to deliver 100 shares of stock at the strike price. When a put is exercised, the seller is required to take delivery of 100 shares at the strike price. Shares are "assigned" (put to the seller).

Intrinsic, Extrinsic, and Time Values Premium

An option premium has three components: intrinsic value, extrinsic value, and time value. The intrinsic value is equal to the number of points that an option is in the money (ITM). This concept is explained in greater detail later in this chapter. The strike is the price at which an option can be exercised; for example, if a call option has a strike price of 45, it provides the buyer the right (but not the requirement) to buy 100 shares at $45 per share. The money rules, or "moneyness," for this example are as follows.

1. If a 45 call is held on stock currently valued at $47 per share, the option is 2 points ITM.
2. If the stock is valued at $45 per share, there is no intrinsic value. This condition—when strike price and stock market value are identical—is called at the money (ATM).
3. If the stock is valued below the strike price, there is no intrinsic value. For example, if the strike price is 45 and the stock is selling at $44 per share, the condition is 1 point out of the money (OTM).

The opposite direction applies to puts. ITM intrinsic value refers to the number of points the stock is below the strike price of the option. For example, if the strike price of a put is 40 and the stock is currently selling at $37 per share, the put option contains 3 points of intrinsic value.

Time value and extrinsic value are the portions of the option premium above and beyond intrinsic value. The longer the time to expiration date, the higher the time value. This value decays over time in a predictable manner, accelerating as expiration nears.

Extrinsic value is the key to identifying option opportunities; it is the volatility premium of the options beyond both intrinsic and time values premium, also called implied volatility.

Long-Term Options and Their Advantages

The LEAPS (Long-term Equity AnticiPation Security) is a long-term contract. In comparison, the standard listed option lasts only about nine months maximum. When various strategies are viewed comparing LEAPS options with listed options, that longer expiration makes a lot of difference to both long and short strategies. There is a far higher time value in a long-term LEAPS option, which exists for up to 30 months. If you purchase options, you must expect to pay more for the longer life of the LEAPS option, because you also buy greater time. For the short seller, the longer period translates to higher income; because as a seller, you receive the premium when you open the short position. For that higher premium income, you must also accept a longer exposure period.

The expiration, more specifically, the time between opening an option position and the expiration date determines the extrinsic value and affects the decisions made on the long side (purchasers) and the short side (sellers).

Strike Price of Options

The strike price is the second feature that determines the option's value. The strike price is fixed and, in the event of exercise, determines the cost or benefit to every option position, whether long or short. The proximity of current market value to the strike price of the option also determines the current premium value and the potential for future gain or loss, as well as the likelihood of exercise. For example, if a call's strike price is 30 (meaning it would be exercised at $30 per share) and the current market value of the stock is $34, the call is 4 points ITM. This option will be exercised in this condition. If the stock's price declines to $28 per share, the call would be 2 points OTM; and if the price stops at the strike price of $30 per share, it is ATM. These conditions are opposite for puts.

Extrinsic value premium is the intangible portion of the premium value. Extrinsic value varies depending on the volatility of the underlying stock.

The Time Advantage for Short Sellers

For the option seller, time is an advantage. The higher the time value premium when the short position is opened, the greater the advantage. If you were to sell a call with 7 points of time value, you could buy to close the position at a profit if the premium value was lower than the original 7 points. For example, if the stock was 5 points higher than the strike price near expiration, you could close the position and avoid exercise—and make a $200 profit ($700 received when the short position was opened, minus $500 paid to close the position—not considering trading fees).

The intrinsic value of the option premium is equal to the number of points and the option is ITM. For example, if your 40 option is held on stock currently valued at $43 per share, the option contains 3 points of intrinsic value. If that call is currently valued at 5 ($500), it consists of $300 intrinsic value and $200 time and extrinsic values. If your put has a strike price of 30 and the stock is valued at 29, the put has 1 point—$100—of intrinsic value because the stock's value is 1 point below the put's strike price. If the current value of the put is 4 ($400), it consists of $100 intrinsic value and $300 time and extrinsic values.

Long and Short

The decision to go long (buy options) or short (sell options) involves analyzing opposite sides of the risk spectrum. Strategies cover the entire range of risk, often only with a subtle change. Long options are disadvantageous in the sense that time works against the buyer; time value disappears as expiration approaches. The less time until expiration, the more difficult it is to profit from buying options; and the longer the time until expiration, the more the speculator must pay to buy contracts. Long options can insure paper profits, but the more popular application of long options is to leverage capital and speculate.

Options present occasional opportunities to take advantage of price swings. When overall market prices fall suddenly, conventional wisdom identifies the occurrence as a buying opportunity; realistically, such price movements make investors fearful, and it is unlikely that many people will willingly place more capital at risk—especially because the paper position of the portfolio is at a loss. Buying options can represent a limited risk for potentially rewarding profits—an opportunity to buy more shares of stock you think of as a long-term hold.

Taking Profits Without Selling Stock

The same argument applies when stock prices rise quickly. Sudden price run-ups are of concern to you as a long-term conservative investor. The dilemma is that you do not want to sell shares and take profits because you want to hold the stock as a long-term investment; at the same time, you expect a price correction. In this situation, you can use long puts to offset price decline.

If you want to hold stock for the long term, you may be willing to ignore short-term price volatility. Even so, few investors can ignore dramatic price movement in their portfolio. When prices plummet or soar, the change in price levels may be only temporary. The tendency for some investors is to sell at the low or to buy at a price peak. In other words, rather than following the wisdom "buy low, sell high," investors often react to short-term trends and "buy high, sell low." You can use options to exploit the market roller coaster. Options can help you deal with price volatility on the upside or the downside for fairly low risk and without losing sight of your long-term investment goals.

The question of speculative versus conservative is not easily addressed. Using options to play market prices is speculative; but at times, you can take advantage of that volatility without selling off shares from your portfolio. The same observation applies on the short side of options, where risks are far different and market strategies vary.

Buyer and Seller Positions Compared

When you short options, you do not have the rights that buyers enjoy. Buyers pay for the right to decide whether to exercise or to sell their long positions. When you are short, you receive payment when you open the position, but someone else decides whether to exercise. Time value works to your advantage in the short position, meaning you control risks while creating a short-term income stream.

The highest risk use of options is the uncovered call. When you sell a call, you receive a premium, but you also accept a potentially unlimited risk. If the stock's market value rises many points and the call is exercised, you will have to pay the difference between the strike price and current market value at the time of exercise. In comparison, the covered call is one of the lowest risk strategies. If you own 100 shares, you can deliver those shares to satisfy exercise, no matter what the market price is. Upon exercise, you keep the premium you were paid.

The capital gain created when a covered call is exercised may produce impressive levels of profit if the basis in stock was lower than the call's strike. In addition, you earn dividends if you continue to own stock.

Understanding Short Seller Risks

The decision to employ options in either long or short positions defines risk profile; the definition of conservative is rarely fixed or inflexible. It is more likely to define an overall level of attitude about specific strategies while acknowledging that strategies may be appropriate in different circumstances. It is a matter of timing a decision based on the current status of the market, your portfolio, and your personal decision to act or to wait out volatile market conditions.

Calls and Call Strategies

If you buy a call or a put option, you have the right to take certain actions in the future, but you do not have an obligation. If you sell a call or a put, the premium you receive as part of an opening transaction is yours to keep, whether the option is later closed, expires, or is exercised.

Options are contracts that grant specific rights to the buyer and impose specific obligations on the seller. If you think of options as intangible contractual, the discussion of how to use options is easier. For example, in a real estate lease option, you have two parts: a lease specifying monthly rent and other terms, and an option. The option fixes the price of the property. If you decide to exercise that option before it expires, you can buy the property at the specified contractual price even if property values are significantly higher.

Stock market options are the same, but they involve options on stock instead of real estate. Every option refers to 100 shares of stock, and options come in two types: calls and puts. When you buy a call, you acquire the right to buy 100 shares of stock at a specific price (the strike price) before the option expires. All options have fixed expiration dates, so the time element of options is a crucial feature to consider when comparing option values. For the buyer, a relatively small risk of capital potentially fixes the price of 100 shares of stock for several months. If that buyer decides to buy the stock, the call can be exercised to acquire 100 shares at a price below current market value. That is the essence of the call.

Is the Strategy Appropriate?

Buying calls is not an appropriate fit in most applications. Buying calls is the best known and most popular option strategy, but it is usually a purely speculative move. If you are convinced that a stock's market value is sure to rise before the expiration of an option, you can buy calls as an alternative to outright purchase of shares. This strategy would be appropriate in the following circumstances.

- You are concerned with short-term price volatility, and you do not want to commit funds to buy shares, but you still want to fix the price of stock at the option's strike price value.
- You want to buy shares, but you do not have funds available now, so buying a relatively cheap call is a sensible alternative (given the chance that you could lose the money).

- You are aware of the risk of loss, and you want to proceed with buying a call anyway, hoping for profits when the price rises.

As with any general rule, there are exceptions. You retain your status as a conservative investor even though circumstances may arise where you want to buy a call. It is not a conservative strategy, but all investment decisions should be driven by circumstances and not by hard-and-fast rules. Although the general rules you set for yourself guide your portfolio decisions, special circumstances and opportunities or limitations can cause exceptions.

Option Terms and Their Meaning

Every call contains a series of terms. These are the type of option, the strike price, the underlying stock, and the expiration date.

The type of option is either a call or a put. The two must be distinguished because they are opposites. All the terms must be specified in an order, including whether you want a call or a put.

The strike price is the price of stock that may be acquired if the option is exercised. This strike price remains unchanged until the option expires, except in cases of stock splits. You have the choice as a buyer of either selling the option to close the position or exercising the option. Upon exercise of a call, you buy shares at the strike price. You "call away" the 100 shares of stock from the call seller. If you exercise a put, you have the right to sell 100 shares, or to "put shares of stock" to the seller and dispose of stock at the fixed strike price.

The underlying stock is the security on which the option is traded. The security cannot be changed; it is fixed. Options are not available on all stocks, but they can be found for most stocks listed on the stock exchanges.

The expiration date is a fixed date in the future specifying when the option expires. This term is critical because after the expiration date, the option no longer exists. As a buyer, you know that the time value premium evaporates if your option is not exercised or sold before the expiration date.

These four terms collectively distinguish every option. None of the terms can be modified or exchanged after you open an option, and the terms determine the option's value (the premium you pay when you open the option).

The Cost of Trading

Augmenting the complexity of buying is the trading expense involved. This applies to both sides of the transaction. You are charged a fee when you open the position and another fee when you close it. In any calculation of risk and potential profit or loss, the cost of trading must be included. If you deal with single-option contracts, you limit your exposure to loss. But at the same time, the per-option cost of trading is higher. Option traders often execute transactions using multiple option contracts. This reduces the per-option cost. But buying options is a high-risk venture and using multiple contracts just to reduce per-option trading costs does not reduce overall risk; it increases the risk, because you must put more capital at risk. For the option buyer, trading costs make the proposition even less likely to turn out profitably. The typical trading fee will be about $5 for trading a single option. Entering and then exiting a trade costs about $10.

As a call buyer, the odds are against you. A second possibility is far more interesting and potentially more profitable: selling calls. Selling stock involves the sequence of events that is opposite from when you go long. You must borrow shares of stock to sell, and opening the short position exposes you to the possibility of loss. If the stock's market value rises, you lose money. Short sellers expect the price of stock to fall. Eventually, they close the position by entering a closing purchase transaction. Short sellers must make enough profit to offset the cost of borrowing stock, trading fees, and the point spread between original selling price and final purchase price.

Selling stock is high risk. If the stock's value rises, you lose money, and short sellers are continually exposed to that market risk. In comparison, using short options is a less expensive alternative to shorting stock.

In, At, or Out of the Money

Selling a call is easier than selling short shares of stock, because you do not have to borrow calls to go short. You simply enter a sell order, and the premium (the value of the call) is placed into your account the following day. When you sell a call in this manner, you are in the same market posture as the short seller of stock, but at less risk. You are hoping that the price of stock will fall so that your short call will lose value. This means you will be able to either close the position profitably with a closing purchase transaction or wait for the call to expire worthless. If the market value of the underlying stock remains at the strike price (ATM) or below the strike price of the call (OTM), exercise will not occur. When the stock's market value is higher than the call's strike price (ITM), you are at risk of exercise. The proximity of the stock's current market value to the strike price is summarized in Figure 2.1.

The option's strike price remains level, but the status of the option relies on stock price movement. This illustrates how a call functions. Whenever the stock's price is higher than the call's strike price, the call is ITM, and whenever the stock's price is below strike price, the call is OTM.

The same logic applies to a put, but the terms are reversed. Referring again to Figure 2.1, if the stock's price was higher than the strike price of the put, it would be OTM, and if the stock's price moved below the strike price, the put would be ITM.

The relationship between strike price and stock price is critical in opening a short position in options. The short-call position can be one of the

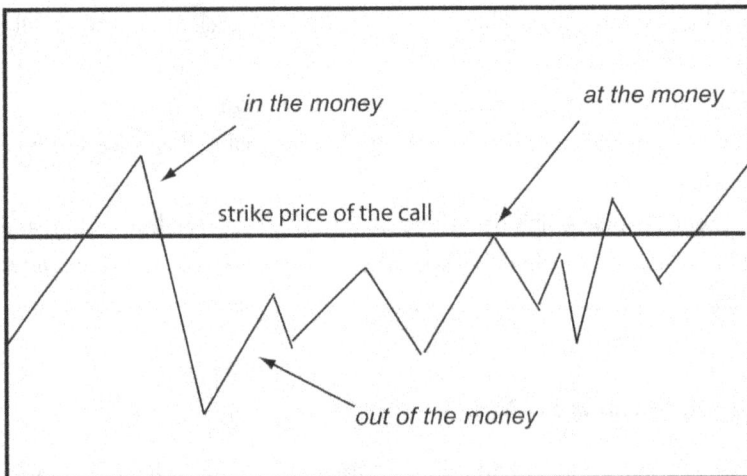

Figure 2.1 Strike price and stock price

highest risk positions. However, it can also be one of the most conservative positions. This riddle is explained by whether you own 100 shares of stock when you sell a call. If you go short with calls and you do not own the stock, risks are theoretically unlimited because the market value of stock can rise indefinitely. This uncovered call strategy is inappropriate for your conservative portfolio. However, when you own 100 shares, those shares are available in the event the call is exercised; in the right circumstances, call selling is highly profitable and conservative. Chapter 3, "Options in Context," compares short calls in these contradictory risk profiles and Chapter 6, "Options as Cash Generators," provide in-depth explanations of covered call-writing strategies, the ultimate conservative use of options.

Puts and Put Strategies

The put is the opposite of the call. If you buy a put, you acquire the right (but not the obligation) to sell 100 shares of the underlying stock. If you exercise a put, you sell 100 shares at that strike price, even if the current market value of stock is far below that level. Like the call, the put expires at a specific date in the future.

As a put buyer, three outcomes are possible.

1. **The put is sold.** You can sell the put at any time prior to expiration. Since time value declines over the holding period, it is a highly speculative strategy to buy puts purely for short-term profits. If you believe that stocks in your portfolio are overbought and you want to protect paper profits, long puts can be used as a form of insurance to protect your stock positions.
2. **The put expires worthless.** If you take no action before the expiration date, the long put becomes worthless, and the entire premium you paid would be a loss. When you buy puts, you profit only if the market value of the underlying stock declines; if the value remains at or above the strike price, your put does not appreciate.
3. **You exercise the put.** If the stock's current market value is far lower than the put's strike price, you have the right to sell 100 shares at the higher strike price. If you own shares of stock and you bought the put for downside protection, exercise can work as a sensible exit strategy.

The Overlooked Value of Puts

The put's strategic potential is easily overlooked by investors and specula-tors. More attention is paid to calls. There are good reasons for this. Short calls can be covered by ownership of 100 shares of stock per call but puts cannot be covered in the same way. The put is more exotic and alien to the mindset of many investors.

Where do puts fit for the conservative investor? Several possible appli-cations of puts are worth considering on both the long and short sides. The best known is the use of long puts for insurance. If you buy one put for every 100 shares of stock, you protect your paper profits; in the event of a decline in the stock's market value, the put's premium value increases. Once the stock's price goes below the put's strike price, loss of stock value is replaced dollar for dollar in higher put premium value.

This protection of paper profits—a form of insurance—is a conserva-tive strategy. You pay a premium for the put because you fear that stock prices have risen too quickly, but you do not want to take profits in the stock. You can use puts in this situation to keep the stock while protect-ing profits. This insurance does not have to be expensive. Just as you can select insurance based on varying levels of deductible and copayment dol-lar values, you can select puts based on their cost and level of protection. You could buy puts at lower strike prices; these would be far cheaper but would provide less protection.

Conservative Guidelines: Selling Puts

Is selling puts a conservative strategy? You must assume several elements to conclude that short puts are appropriate in your conservative portfolio:

- **The strike price is a fair price for the stock.** Whenever you short a put, you must accept the possibility that the put will be exercised. You must accept the strike price as a price you are willing to pay for the stock.
- **The premium you receive justifies the exposure.** When you sell options, you are paid the premium. That premium and the length of time you remain exposed to possible exercise must justify the decision.

- **The risk range is minimal.** When you consider the spread between the put's strike price and your estimated support price for the stock, minus the put premium, how many points remain?

The uncovered put has the same market risk as the covered call, making short puts conservative and in many cases, preferable to covered calls, because you do not need to own the underlying stock to write short puts.

Listed Options and LEAPS Options

Traditionally, risk assessment for options is based on a short lifespan—eight months or less for listed options. The ever-growing popularity of LEAPS—long-term options that last if 30 months—changes the analysis. Even for the long position, the risk of ever-declining time value takes on a different context when looking two or two and half years ahead.

The availability of long-term options makes long positions more viable in many more situations. Longer-term options contain far greater time value, of course, because time value is just that the value of time. So, compared with a six- or eight-month time span, a 24- to 30-month option has far greater potential—for both long and short positions.

Using Long Calls in Volatile Markets

The not-uncommon situation of a volatile market makes it difficult even for conservative investors to time their decisions. It could make sense to buy LEAPS calls instead of stock. As an initial risk analysis, you cannot lose more than the premium cost of the LEAPS call, so the initial market risk is lower. At the same time, in going long with calls, you acquire the right (but not the obligation) to buy 100 shares of the underlying stock at any time before expiration. If the LEAPS call has 30 months to go, a lot can happen between now and then.

The risk is that the stock's market value will not rise, or even if it does, it may not rise enough to offset the cost of time value and to appreciate adequately to justify your investment. The solution allows you to reduce the cost of buying the LEAPS call by selling calls on the same stock. If the

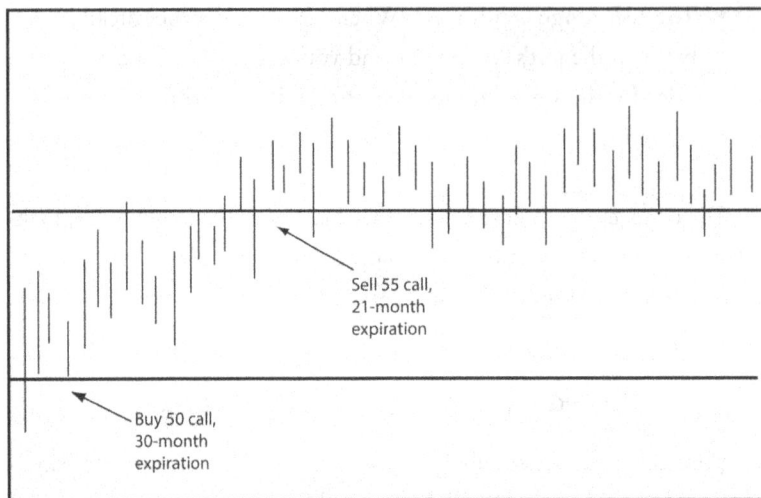

Sell 55 call,
21-month
expiration

Buy 50 call,
30-month
expiration

Figure 2.2 Long- and short-call strategy

short calls expire before the long LEAPS call, and if the short call's strike prices are higher than the strike price of the long call, there is no market risk. A likely scenario in this "covered option" position is that the short call's time value will decline; it can be closed at a profit and replaced with another short call. It is possible, based on ideal price movement of the underlying stock, that your premium income from selling short calls can repay the entire cost of the long-term long LEAPS position. There are no guarantees, but it is possible.

The basic long–short LEAPS strategy is summarized in Figure 2.2.

This strategy has two legs. First, you purchase a long call with a 50 strike price, and later, you sell a 55 call. To avoid an uncovered short position, the 55 call must expire at the same time as the long call, or before. If the short call outlasts the long call, you face a period in which that short call will be uncovered.

Using LEAPS Puts in a Covered Capacity

Long LEAPS puts can also be part of a two-step strategy. For example, you purchase LEAPS puts for insurance on existing long stock positions and reduce your insurance cost by selling puts that expire sooner than the LEAPS put and have lower strike prices. This basic strategy—

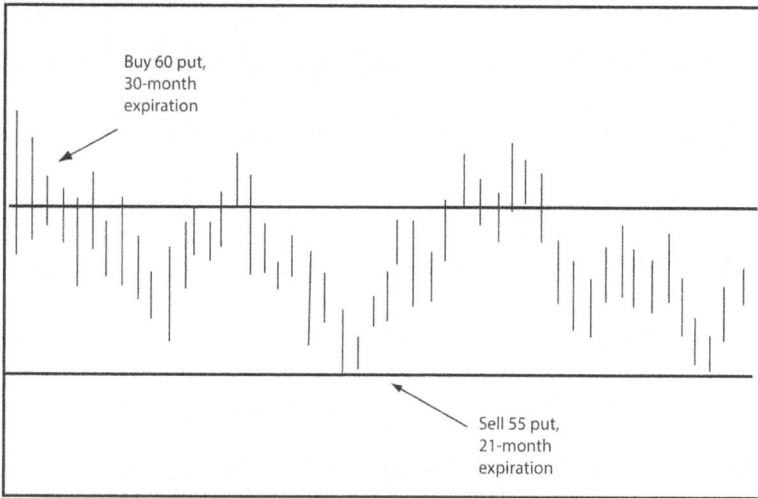

Buy 60 put,
30-month
expiration

Sell 55 put,
21-month
expiration

Figure 2.3 Long- and short-put strategy

combining long puts and covering them with short puts—is summarized in Figure 2.3.

The purpose in covering the put is to reduce the risk of exercise and resulting loss, and at the same time, to reduce the cost of buying the long put. These strategies—covering long options with shorter-term short positions—work best when your estimate of likely price movement in the stock is correct. The wisdom of using either strategy is based on your ability to read intermediate-term volatility trends accurately. The strategies make long positions in options more practical than the purely speculative approach, but profitability is not ensured. The overall purpose of the long option strategy is to maximize the opportunity while identifying worst-case outcomes and setting up the strategies so that you will not lose or so that losses are minimal.

Limiting Your Strategies to Conservative Plays

The basic premise for conservative options trading is: Any strategy should be used only on stocks with sound fundamentals that you bought for their value, not used simply to write options with high volatility. The existence of strong fundamental value in the stock, long-term growth, dividend income, and repetitive options trades maximizes the conservative strategy.

Risk levels of the underlying stock may increase since original purchase date, possibly a signal that the underlying should be reevaluated. Should you sell that stock and find an alternative issue with lower volatility levels? You may be better off respecting your conservative stock standards based on fundamental analysis, writing options with "typical" pricing, and staying away from stocks and options with higher than average volatility.

The idea of avoiding stocks and options with higher than average implied that volatility makes sense in your conservative portfolio. If you restrict your activity to long stock positions, you monitor your portfolio constantly. If the fundamentals change, you replace your hold position with a sell. Not only should that standard be retained, but the implied volatility in option premium can serve as a red flag, enabling you to check other indicators to decide whether you want to keep your long stock position.

Identifying Quality of Earnings

The last word in picking options is that quality of earnings mandates the quantifications of a stock.[1] The fundamentals apply only to the stock because options have no tangible value. When the option's implied volatility changes from the norm, it happens for a reason. It is a symptom and perhaps a signal that the fundamental strength (the quality of earnings) of the stock has changed as well. Anticipation is the spark of the stock market, and more decisions are made in anticipation of future risk, profit, and other change than on any known fundamentals. In adhering to your conservative standards, a highly volatile option premium may be a more cautionary sign than a covered call opportunity.

---

[1]   Quality of earnings refers to the fundamental strength of the corporation and to its long-term growth potential. A high quality of earnings translates to greater prospects for long-term growth and fewer unpleasant earnings surprises. One definition of this term is "The amount of earnings attributable to higher sales or lower costs rather than artificial profits created by accounting anomalies such as inflation of inventory" (www.investopedia.com).

The next chapter provides an overview of risk assessment in terms of return calculations and explains the many ways to calculate returns.

Class questions for discussion and/or mini-case studies

Multiple choice

1. A conservative use of options includes:
   a. Uncovered call and put trading.
   b. Covered puts.
   c. Hedging of equity positions.
   d. All of the above.
2. There are three forms of value in options. These are:
   a. Extrinsic, intrinsic, and time values.
   b. Long-term, short-term, and perceived values.
   c. Intrinsic, time, and actual values.
   d. Volatility, risk, and time values.
3. The risk in an uncovered call is:
   a. Too great to be part of a conservative strategy.
   b. Determined by whether the underlying security is owned.
   c. Identical to market risk of a covered call.
   d. Nonexistent because exercise will never occur.

Exercise for Discussion

Find an options listing for a stock and identify the levels of risk based on distance between the underlying price and the strike price of the option. Explain why these risks vary and identify the contract with the most conservative attributes.

CHAPTER 3

Options in Context

Any investment strategy—from plain to exotic—contains specific attributes and can be defined in terms of risk, rates of return, and strategies for changing market conditions. Options are probably the most flexible investment products available. You can use them alone, in combination with other options, or as hedge devices to protect stock positions. Options can help you to exploit market price swings, and you can utilize them in speculative or conservative ways.

The Nature of Risk and Reward

Any assessment of an investment decision has to involve a study of risk and reward. Your conservative approach to investing is based on your sensitivity to risk as a primary means for all your decisions. You are less likely than the typical investor to react to sudden market changes out of panic or greed; your view is long term. Rather than watching index-based and volume trends every day, you track a company's fundamentals. You base your decisions on earnings reports, capital strength, and operating trends. The stocks you currently hold will be sold if and when you determine that the fundamental strength of the company has changed or if you locate another company whose stock is a better candidate for long-term growth and safety.

When options are involved, the risk equation changes. You are likely not only to alter your investing profile to take options-based risks in some circumstances, but also to use options to protect paper profits without selling or to reduce your basis in stock to create downside protection. The appropriate use of options can increase the conservative nature of your portfolio because some strategies protect existing positions against loss.

Using Volatility as a Risk Measurement

The usual method for defining market risk of stocks involves price volatility. This is a starting point. The more erratic the price trend, the greater the risk and the more difficulty you will have in trying to forecast future price movement. When a stock's trading range is broad, it further complicates the picture; price volatility is a problem for stock investors because owning shares in a volatile company means valuation is on an unending roller coaster ride.

Price volatility in a stock naturally affects option premium value as well. The greater a stock's price volatility, the greater the volatility in option premium. The definition of what constitutes a conservative investment varies; it works only when stock has been selected on a conservative basis as a starting point. You may need to accept lower premium levels and lower implied volatility in exchange for safer overall portfolio positions.

The interaction between risk and opportunity is a fact of life. The higher the risk, the higher potential returns; the lower the risk, the lower those returns. Example: You are reviewing available options on McDonald's (MCD). The market value of stock was at $197.60 at the time, so you are reviewing 195 and 197.50 calls. Clearly, your selection of options will be based on your purchase price for the stock. If you pay $196 for shares, the 195 call is not as attractive as the 197.50 call. Upon exercise, you would experience a $1 capital loss on the 195 call, or a $1.50 gain on the 197.50 call. The selection of an appropriate covered call has to

Figure 3.1 Selling calls in a rising market

Source: Chart coutesy of StockCharts.com

include a critical analysis of your basis in stock, which makes the point that if your original basis in stock is far below either option, you must make comparisons based on exercise with the certainty of profits. A study of the current 14-day options reveals that the 197.50 call is available at 2.11 ($211) and the 195 call is going for 3.70 ($370). Your selection of either one must consider the capital gain, because appropriate strike levels have to be selected based on your original cost of the stock. Exercise of the 95 creates a capital loss of $100 ($196 purchase minus 195 strike) versus premium of $211. Exercise of the 197.50 creates a capital gain of $150 plus option premium of $211 (net profit of $361).

Selling calls in this situation, when the value of stock is on the rise, is a sensible use of options, with profits more likely than losses. The status of MCD is summarized in Figure 3.1. The trend—prices moving higher—is highlighted with a trend line.

Using Technical Analysis as a Risk Measurement

An alternative to the analysis of implied volatility is the study of stock charts. In this method, you study the chart of the underlying stock and look for reversal and confirmation signals to time option trades.

The advantage in this method is that seeking two or more exceptionally strong reversal signals may offer a better than average outcome. No one is going to be right 100 percent of the time, but chart analysis can be very effective in identifying strength or weakness in a current price trend. Chart analysis requires confirmation in the form of a second indicator, foreshadowing the same likelihood of reversal in the near future. If you can find three or four indicators, it further strengthens the chances for good timing.

The first disadvantage in technical analysis of stock charts is that this is a complex process. It can be simplified with practice and observation over time, but for anyone who are not familiar with technical analysis the process can be daunting. The second disadvantage is the skepticism many investors have toward technical analysis. Does it really work? It does work in the sense that price strength or weakness tends to show up in the form of specific indicators, but interpreting these accurately is a very subjective process.

Using both fundamental and technical analysis strengthens the overall quality of information. Focusing only on one side or the other has inherent weaknesses. By combining both, your starting point is a prequalified value investment. By selecting stocks on the basis of long-term dividend growth, stable debt ratio, and growing revenue and earnings, you know that the companies you pick are strong in a fundamental sense. The technical tests identify volatility in price trends and if and when reversal signals are located, it will give you a form on insight about price trends not possible with fundamental analysis.

Options Used to Mitigate Stock Investment Risk

With well-selected stocks, the option premium is likely to be "in the zone" of expectation; in other words, the low risk of the conservatively picked stock reflects the same low volatility of the option. You gain the advantage, even when dealing with safe stocks and options, in three ways:

1. **You select longer-term option writes.** The LEAPS call creates significant profit potential in the covered call strategy. You want to use OTM calls to avoid exercise. When you use LEAPS calls, premium levels often are high enough that the simple yield is more attractive than traditional listed options because of time. The greater the time left until expiration, the higher the time value.

2. **The selection of covered writes is limited to stock that has appreciated.** It would be contrary to your goals to write covered calls with strike prices close to your original basis in the stock. Some of the best premium returns are found in calls whose current market value is close to the call's strike price. The covered call write is a means for taking profits and providing downside protection, but without necessarily selling the stock. The strategy solves the dilemma every stockholder faces: Stock has appreciated, and the temptation is to take profits, but you don't want the capital gain and you don't want to give up the long-term investment.

3. **Exercise is avoided with rolling techniques.** You want to repeat the cash profits from writing covered calls on appreciated stock. The best of all worlds is to keep a strong long-term growth stock while

generating repetitive option profits. If the short call is exercised, you would gladly accept the high yields, but at the same time, you prefer to avoid exercise. Risk of exercise should not be overlooked; however, as it can occur at any time the short option is open.

Lost Opportunity Risk and Options

Another form of risk to consider is lost opportunity risk. If the stock's price soars far above the strike price of the covered call, you lose your shares through exercise. Your stock has to be sold at the fixed strike price when that strike price is below the current market value.

Is writing covered calls worth the lost opportunity risk? You will probably have calls exercised periodically, and you will wish you had waited so that you could have benefited from the higher stock price. But your portfolio profits will be higher from writing covered calls on appreciated stock than they will be from simply keeping your long positions without options activity. The lost opportunity is the exception rather than the rule because, by definition, a conservative selection of stocks creates consistent price trends (low volatility) and less likelihood of sudden and unexpected price changes (high volatility). You can further mitigate or even eliminate the risk of exercise using rolling techniques once you have short options.

Perceptions About Options

Properly employed, options can strengthen your portfolio and provide greater protection than just holding well-selected stocks. Because prices tend to move in cycles, short-term and intermediate-term pricing may be erratic, and even the best-chosen stocks go through reversal and consolidation patterns.

As long as long-term fundamental signals continue to show strength, the conservative philosophy is to hold and accumulate stock and wait out the market. This traditional approach observes correctly that short-term pricing is unpredictable as an indicator. Short-term price movement is not useful for long-term prediction. However, it remains possible to (a) protect paper profits and even take those profits without selling shares, (b) exploit market price overreactions, and (c) generate current returns, all without taking on added market risks. The lost opportunity risk associated with committing shares of stock to a fixed strike price should be evaluated along with the rates of return, the value of downside protection, and the yield diversification you achieve with the use of options in a conservative manner.

Strategic Timing and Short-Term Price Changes

Consider the possibilities in options trading when markets are exceptionally volatile. Most of your capital may be tied up in long stock positions that would produce losses if sold when market prices are low. You recognize that this is the time to buy more stock, but you are uncertain, and you do not have capital available to make a bold move even if you wanted to. This is the perfect opportunity—using a limited amount of capital, of course—to buy cheap calls. You know that sharp market drops usually and rebounds quickly. You also recognize the stocks whose fundamental strength supports the probability of a healthy return to the normal trading range. Picking the bargains is not difficult; the decision to put money into the market at these moments is the difficult part.

When your portfolio is depressed, you have three choices. First, you can sell everything and just get out of the market. Second, you can wait out the cycle and hope prices rebound. Third, you can seek a rescue strategy to regain lost value as quickly as possible. This is where options can play a key role. For example, as of the end of 2010, thousands of investors had paper losses in their personal portfolio as well as in their retirement plans. This is a distressing situation; at the time, no one had any idea of how long it would take for the market to recover; some people thought it never would. Uncertainty in the economy, politics, and the market itself, all worked together to increase the fear investors experienced.

Being conservative does not mean that you have the same attitude in all market conditions. Flexibility is an essential tool in your portfolio management arsenal. When opportunities present themselves, it is prudent to take them. If you lack the capital to buy shares, or you are fearful of further price declines, options present the perfect compromise. You can limit your risk by investing only a small amount of capital; and the timing can work to your advantage given the likely price patterns in big-number changes.

This does not suggest that you should speculate in long calls. But every conservative investor has survived through big price swings and seen the results—a big drop followed by a period of uncertainty and then a rapid return to previous levels. This trend can take a few days, weeks, or even months to play out.

Short Positions: Naked or Covered

The concept of speculating on long calls or puts is contrary to the generally understood definition of conservative. There may be moments when you want to use long calls or long puts to take advantage of price changes. It may be appropriate, given the timing, and may even conform to your conservative standards.

Some strategies involving short calls and puts may also conform to your conservative risk profile based on prevailing market conditions and your portfolio positions. The basic covered calls strategy is the most obvious example. When you sell a call, you are taking paper profits and reducing your basis in the stock; you expose yourself to the possibility of losing future price gains in exchange for the certainty of premium income today.

The Uncovered Call: A Violation of the Conservative Theme, Usually

Is it ever justified to sell uncovered calls? In the conservative philosophy, it is not. Uncovered calls are one of the highest risk strategies possible. Chapter 9 contains an example of one situation in which writing uncovered calls can work for a conservative portfolio: the ratio write.

One technique involves topping off a ratio write with one long call. In effect, this eliminates the uncovered portion of the ratio write. For example, if you own 300 shares, full coverage involves selling three calls. If you sell four calls, you have a ratio write. This can also be viewed as the combination of three covered calls and one uncovered call. However, you can further modify this position by purchasing a single call with a higher strike price. In effect, this creates a different kind of combination: a covered call strategy on 300 shares accompanied by a spread (a strategy in which the benefits of one side of the position are offset by the risk in the other). As long as the modified ratio write can be accomplished with a net credit (money coming in rather than going out), the risk is limited. The difference in strike prices between the fourth short call and the long call is a risk if and when the stock moves about the highest short call strike price. Chapter 9 examines this modified strategy in greater detail.

Covered calls are related to ownership of stock, so exercise risk is easily controlled. Short puts are a different matter. In many instances, writing puts makes sense. Because puts cannot be covered in the same way as calls, it is easy to overlook the potential of writing uncovered puts or covering them by combining a short put with later-expiring long puts. The risks of short puts are far more limited than those of short calls, because the potential decline in value is finite. Uncovered puts have the same market risk as covered calls, making them very conservative.

Margin Requirements

There are two areas in which option investors have to live with special rules: taxes and trading restrictions. The tax rules are covered later; a more immediate concern involves the special financial requirements that apply once you move beyond the status of stockholder and begin to make actual option trades.

Margin rules are intended to limit the volume of trading undertaken by investors with limited capital. The Securities and Exchange Commission (SEC) defines a pattern day trader as any individual who makes four or more day trades within five business days. A day trade is opening and closing a position within a single day. Once you make the fourth-day trade within a five-day period, you are required to maintain at least $25,000 equity in your account (in cash and securities). For many options traders, the restriction certainly applies. Unless you can limit activity to three or fewer trades, you will be treated as a pattern day trader.

The problem is not severe by itself, but having that label removed could pose a problem. Your broker may view you and your account as a potential problem and there is no automatic system for every broker to remove the label of pattern day trader. At the very least, you will be required to submit a letter promising not to repeat the trading levels of the past. Your broker may also suspend your account if you violate that promise. Even when pattern day trading does not do great damage to the broker or increases its market risks, being labeled as a pattern day trader can inhibit your ability to trade options freely.

Other Margin Rules

All investors must be concerned with the initial margin (the amount of value required at the time a position is opened) and with maintenance margin requirements (additional margin required if prices change in the securities involved).

Options traders must be aware of these margin rules for options trading. The term "margin" relating to stock trades is far different than its definition for options. As a stock trader, margin is a borrowing mechanism. For example, you can borrow up to 50 percent of the basis in stock. But for options, margin refers to collateral that must be on deposit for certain types of options trades. The strategies involving options may look good on paper but, given margin requirements, limited capital could make combinations of positions impractical.

The margin rules are complex for advanced trading strategies and combinations. To see a complete summary of a typical broker's margin requirements, check the Chicago Board Options Exchange (CBOE) free download of the "Margin Manual" at https://cboe.com/learncenter/pdf/margin2-00.pdf

Given the limitation on pattern day trading and the capital requirements, it would be difficult for an investor to become active in options without placing substantial capital at risk. With options, the threshold of four trades could be crossed quickly and easily within a few days, at least occasionally; it is the nature of options trading to execute a number of trades in a short period of time because market conditions present immediate opportunities.

Return Calculations: Seeking Valid Comparisons

Margin limitations inhibit investor activity if only a small amount of capital is available. An equally complex problem is the calculation of returns from option activity. In attempting to measure and compare option trades—whether employing timing strategies or the safer and more reliable covered call—you face a problem. How do you measure your profits? Consider the problem of the covered call trade. You have three possible outcomes: exercise, expiration, and closing the position. In the first instance, you combine a capital gain with profits from selling a covered call; in the second, you realize a level of profit, but you still own the stock. You cannot compare possible returns on a like-kind basis. Excluding capital gains on stock is always suggested; however, in picking a strike, you should be aware of your basis in the stock and limit your covered calls to strikes that, if exercised, will produce a net profit and not a net loss.

Return if exercised is calculated as a percentage of the stock's value, either at the time the strategy is entered into or based on the strike value. Using the strike value makes the most sense because that is the price at which stock will be called away. Your capital gain on stock depends on your basis and should be calculated separately. As long as you purchased the stock at a price below the short call's strike price, you can ensure a capital gain in the event of exercise.

Limiting this discussion to the option-only return allows you to compare the various option outcomes. While return if exercised (also termed if-called rate of return) appears to be the best possible return on a short strategy, it is not always the case. To make return comparisons valid, you have to view them on an annualized basis. When you consider the possibility of a short call simply expiring worthless (or being closed at a profit), you can repeat the strategy. The ability to sell covered calls repeatedly turns stock into a combined long-term growth instrument and current cash cow. The combined annual income from dividends and call premiums can make nonexercised returns far more advantageous than the exercised rate of return. Including dividends in the calculation of covered call return (termed "total" rate of return) is essential; with all other factors identical, the difference in dividend yield often makes one stock more favorable than another. Dividend yield represents a major portion of overall covered call return.

Table 3.1 Market data for covered calls

Stock name	Symbol	Share price *	Strike	Premium	%	Annualized**
AT&T	T	$30.34	30.50	1.02	3.34%	21.39%
Southern Co.	SO	52.44	52.50	0.94	1.79	11.46
Altria	MO	51.41	52.50	1.29	2.46	15.75

* Closing prices as of April 25, 2019. Source: Charles Schwab & Co.
** To annualize, divide yield by the number of days to expiration and then multiply by 365.

To begin analyzing various options and their potential returns, a side-by-side comparison between stocks is useful, and for each stock, potential outcome (exercise, expiration, or close) is studied. Table 3.1 summarizes the market data for the three companies in the model portfolio. These are based on the 57-day options at the strike immediately above market value of each stock. Even though the same time to expiration is employed, considerable differences will be found for each stock. A careful and thorough comparative analysis of covered call candidates is needed in order to make an informed selection.

Annualizing each outcome produces the yield that would be realized if the position were held open for exactly one year. Using the yields is reported in Table 3.1.

AT&T	3.34% ÷ 57 days x 365 days = 21.39%
Southern Co.	1.79% ÷ 57 days x 365 days = 11.46%
Altria	2.46% ÷ 57 days x 365 days = 15.75%

These examples compare calls OTM. Because all options in this example expire 57 days from the study date, the percentages shown are comparable; but annualized return, while equally comparable, tells the real story and allows you to make comparisons between these three companies.

The return you can expect to earn on any one option depends on the premium's relationship to the current price and should include dividend yield on the stock. The calculation of option returns also has to consider the ramifications of exercise. Although you do not complicate your analysis by including this factor, it is clear that differences will occur. For example, when the annualized yield is adjusted to include dividends, the picture

Table 3.2 Annualized return with dividend yield

Stock name	Symbol	Annualized	Dividend yield	Total return
AT&T	T	21.39%	6.64%	28.03
Southern Co.	SO	11.46	4.66	16.12
Altria	MO	15.75	5.95	21.70

* Closing prices as of April 25, 2019. Source: Charles Schwab & Co.

is changed considerably. Table 3.2 is based on the assumption that annualized return (a holding period of exactly one year) is comparable, and that this should be adjusted to reflect one year of dividend yield as well.

This calculation demonstrates that it is not reliable to simply compare potential returns on covered calls. You also have to consider dividend yield, especially if you are going to select one stock over another as the stock to buy.

Return If Exercised

Although exercise could occur at any time the call is ITM, you cannot accurately compare the yield unless you make this assumption. Return varies based on the time the option is left open.

Stock price can also be deceiving in the side-by-side analysis. All comparisons involving 57-day calls set up annualized returns on a comparative basis. To continue evaluating the portfoliowide returns in these cases, you need to track also the dividend income and growth in the stock's market value. However, for option-specific returns, the results vary considerably, not only due to different dividend yields but also based on varying times to expiration.

Dividend yield affects overall profitability and may also influence which stocks you would use for the covered call strategy. The most sensible approach is perhaps to calculate both with and without dividend yield and then compare outcomes.

Return If Expired

Comparing return if exercised to return if expired is useful because it shows the result of two possible outcomes. However, it is not accurate to compare the two outcomes to decide which is preferable. The covered call is sensible only if any of the possible outcomes would be justified and acceptable, but consider the problem of trying to compare exercise to expiration. Upon exercise, your stock is called away, then you have a taxable capital gain, and that is going to vary depending on the strike you pick versus your original basis in the stock. In the case of expiration, you continue to own stock. You are free to repeat the covered call strategy after expiration. This means your yield can recur repeatedly as long as exercise never happens, so a true overall comparison is not really possible. Given the potential for repetitive returns from the covered call strategy, the rate of turnover becomes important. The more often you can replace a current covered call with another, the higher your premium income.

It is valid to compare the potential return to the stock's current value. You must own the stock to enter the covered call strategy as a requirement under your conservative risk profile. Comparing yield to your original cost makes it outdated, because there is no relationship between today's covered call strike price and your original purchase price. The validity of comparing expiration returns to today's price rests with the assumption that you would select one or more covered calls based on (a) proximity between strike price of the call and today's market price, (b) related premium levels, and (c) time until expiration. The major difference between the two potential outcomes (exercise and expiration) is whether you continue to own the stock at the end of the strategy. This is where capital gains and dividend yield become important.

Dividend yield has to be an important component in the selection of stocks for covered call writing, whether you currently own the stock or are considering purchasing shares in the future. You may pursue high-yielding stocks to increase returns, or you may avoid writing covered calls to preserve dividend yield. Another alternative is to write ITM covered calls on high-dividend stocks, while avoiding exposure in ex-dividend month (thus avoiding early exercise). The idea is to exploit time value and either close at a profit or allow the position to expire if the stock price declines (or even to accept exercise when the capital loss is much smaller than the call premium, due to high time value when the position is opened).

Expiration might be the worst-case scenario if it yields the lower return compared with closing or having stock called away. But you have control. You do not need to keep option positions open until expiration. By comparing if-expired returns to the alternative of closing positions today and replacing them with richer premium short calls, consider the following:

- The net yield, on an annualized basis, of closing the call. This is the difference between the original sales premium and the current closing purchase premium, net of transaction expenses, calculated on an annualized basis.
- The comparative yield on a new short call, given longer time to expiration, higher time value premium, and proximity between strike price and current market value.
- The increase, if any, in the strike price level. If the stock's market value is higher today than when you sold the original call, consider selling calls with higher strike prices. This increases your capital gain in the event of exercise, yet it keeps your position OTM and maintains your conservative standard for covered call writing.

With these variables in mind, the worst case is difficult to quantify. Since the comparison is not valid between stocks, it is not accurate to assign a preference of one outcome over another. All the factors—including exercise, dividend yield, and capital gains—have to be considered as part of your analysis. The original cost of stock, proximity between cost and strike price, and proximity between current value and strike price affect your decision, and those factors are going to vary between stocks.

Long-Term Goals as a Guiding Force

Working within a conservative framework is not always an absolute or easily defined criterion for how to invest or what products to select. Your level of conservatism changes with market circumstances. The various options strategies enable you to take advantage of market high points without disposing of stock you prefer to keep. Degrees of conservatism are possible and may not be fixed. It might be considered conservative to use options at market extremes as long as large amounts of capital are not risked or exercise of short positions produces an undesirable outcome. This is an individual decision, and no universal standard can identify whether it is appropriate.

Current circumstances affect how you invest, and they should. It is not conservative to invest in the same manner in every situation. You need strategies for managing your portfolios in down markets as well as in up markets, and options in their various configurations are powerful tools for protecting your long-term positions and for identifying and taking profit opportunities without compromising your goals.

There is a tendency to classify specific options strategies universally, so taking long positions is always thought to be high risk, and writing covered positions is always viewed as safe. Neither of these is always true. For example, writing covered calls is ill-advised when the stock price is depressed, especially if the current price of an underlying stock is lower than your basis. If you think prices are going to climb in the future to reverse the downtrend, timing of the covered call write would be poor.

Exercise as a Desirable Outcome

One aspect of options often ignored is the desirability of exercise in some circumstances. Exercise is usually avoided as part of an overall strategic approach based on your wanting to enhance current income while doing all you can to keep well-selected, long-term growth stocks. In the covered call strategy, exercise is most likely when the stock's price is rising, so escaping exercise provides more capital gains in the stock, to be realized later. Avoiding exercise by rolling out of positions is a practical method for managing covered call positions; even if exercise does occur in the future, it is always preferable at a higher strike price. In the following circumstances, you will welcome exercise:

- **Writing deep ITM calls, even with tax consequences in mind.** If you have a substantial carryover loss to bring forward, you are limited to a maximum of $3,000 per year in capital losses you can claim. When your carryover is far above that level, you will not be concerned about the loss of long-term status you suffer when writing deep ITM covered calls. In fact, in that situation, your covered-call-writing strategy could be designed to invite exercise.

- **Selling puts as a form of contingent purchase when the strike price makes sense.** If you are willing to buy stock at the short put strike price, minus the premium, exercise is a desirable outcome.
- **Accepting exercise when fundamental indicators have changed.** You may find yourself in the interesting position of owning stock with a short covered call, also to discover that you no longer want to own the stock. If the call is ITM, you can simply accept exercise in this situation and take your profit. Inviting exercise is one method of dealing with ever-changing market conditions.

As a conservative investor, you continually struggle with the problem of market volatility. Even when you believe stock is worth holding for the long term, how can you ensure that today's paper profits are not lost in future market price movements? You can use several conservative strategies to accomplish these defensive goals. As Chapter 4 demonstrates, even the technical practice of chart analysis can be incorporated as part of a very conservative system for portfolio management based on options strategies.

Class questions for discussion and/or mini-case studies

Multiple choice

1. Risk can be measured through:
   a. Financial analysis alone.
   b. Technical analysis alone.
   c. Volatility in equities or technical analysis.
   d. Volatility alone.
2. Uncovered calls are considered:
   a. High risk in most situations.
   b. Generally low risk.
   c. The best way to generate cash in a portfolio.
   d. As illegal under current securities law.
3. Annualizing return is accomplished by:
   a. Estimating future income out to a full year's holding period.

b. Assuming a one-year holding period in every situation.

c. Dividing net return by the number of days held, and then multiplying by 365.

d. Looking back at the past year to calculate annual returns.

Discussion

Locate a stock chart presenting the ideal circumstances for writing covered calls. Explain why the situation is favorable and the range of possible outcomes expected.

CHAPTER 4

Chart-Based Analysis

An options trading program can be based on the combined use of fundamental analysis of companies and technical analysis of stock prices. These two approaches to investing and trading complement one another by providing a broader perspective on value and risk.

Trading options based on the timing of entry or exit can be accomplished effectively, not to attempt to profit 100 percent of the time, but to improve occurrences of profitable timing above the average.

Criteria for Chart-Based Analysis

Four key criteria should be applied to chart analysis. These are:

1. *Limit yourself to fundamentally sound companies*

The starting point for every conservative portfolio is the disciplined selection of its components. Managers set criteria for investments to include in the portfolio, and ultimately the success of investment activity depends on how well you can stay with those criteria and avoid the temptation to take risks beyond your carefully defined limits.

2. *Seek adequate reversal and confirmation*

It is not enough to simply spot a reversal signal. No portfolio decisions should be based on single indicators. You need to ensure that a signal is confirmed independently before acting; and two or more forms of confirmation are desirable. Finding reversal and confirmation in the underlying security leads to a determination of which options to trade based on those signals. A related and equally important guideline is not to act if you don't find those signals; the purpose of finding reversal and confirmation is to improve your chances of well-timed entry and exit.

3. *Seek many different forms of confirmation*

If you use many different indicators in combination to find points for entry and exit, you improve the likelihood of profits. Traders tend to identify a very short list of favorite indicators and look only for those, without being able to expand the search horizon. This is a mistake. The more indicators you locate to spot reversals and confirm them, the better your overall outcome is likely to be, and the higher the experience of profits over losses.

4. *Diversify in terms of dollar amounts traded*

You might be able to create a nicely diversified portfolio of equity positions but overlook the importance of limiting risks through the dollar amount traded. For example, if you set a limit of $1,000 per trade on long positions, you never place more than $1,000 at risk. The mistake traders make is to set the rule and then violate it. They see what looks like a great opportunity and put in $7,000; it turns out to be one of those poorly timed traded that everyone has from time to time. As a form of diversification, keeping the trading levels the same for each trade makes sense and is really the only way to manage the market risk of buying and selling options—even with conservative strategies.

Finding Fundamentally Sound Companies

Criteria for picking stocks can be applied as a starting point. Chapter 13 examines in detail a sample of five criteria: revenue and earnings, capitalization and working capital, PE ratio, core earnings, and dividend yield.

All of these criteria should be studied as trends. Analyzing the 10-year history of these criteria reveals the strength or weakness of the company on a fundamental basis; no one-year status or results can tell the whole story. When the fundamentals are added to technical analysis, you build a strong portfolio of value investments that also offer strong growth potential.

Using Many Different Reversal Indicators in Combination

The key to chart analysis is to use many indicators in combination. Relying on any single indicator is dangerous because an indicator, by itself, is not adequate to generate entry or exit.

You need at least two separate indicators revealing the same likely next change in price; preferably, having even more is better. A collection of many indicators is always stronger than any one signal by itself.

There are points in the trading range at which many indicators have more significance than other points. When the price is near resistance or support, reversal becomes more likely than at any other point in the trading range. When price moves above resistance or below support, reversal is even more likely to occur. This is true when the breakout occurs with strong reversal signals, including price gaps, candlesticks, or double tops and bottoms.

Diversification in Terms of Dollar Amounts Traded

Conservative portfolio management involves two attributes that might seem to contradict one another at first glance. First is the desirable selection of strong value companies as portfolio components on a buy-and-hold basis or at least for more than just a speculative in-and-out move. Second is the idea that on a technical basis, you might move in and out of positions when price trends turn or when the fundamentals change.

Fundamentals change occurs and should not be ignored. For example, a profitable company loses market share or peaks out and begins losing profits, a troubling change. Or a once equity-based company loses profits and begins capitalizing its operations using long-term debt, another dangerous change in the fundamentals. When the profitability and capitalization picture began to change, the smart move is to sell and look for stronger alternatives.

A Study of Charts for the Model Portfolio

The three stocks in the model portfolio qualify on a fundamental basis, based on a review of revenue and earnings, PE range, dividend yield, and capitalization (as measured by the debt to total capitalization ratio). However, on a technical basis, all these stocks go through periods of bullish and bearish trends. Using options, you can have the best of both worlds: keeping a portfolio of value investments for the long term and applying conservative options strategies to time trades based on movement and reversal of trends.

To show how this works, the following section is a summary of the three companies and an analysis of their three-month stock charts as of April 25, 2019. Included in the indicators besides price are:

- Bollinger Bands, a volatility indicator of three bands, a middle line representing a 20-period moving average; and an upper and lower band representing two standard deviations from the middle line.[1] The distinction "20, 2" reveals that the chart's Bollinger Bands represent 20 periods and 2 standard deviations. When price moves higher than the upper band or lower than the lower band, it signals that the price level has moved out of range, and a correcting change is likely.
- Volume, which is useful for spotting likely reversal timing. When you see a volume spike, it identifies a likely moment when the current trend is about to be exhausted and a reversal is likely to follow.
- Relative Strength Index (RSI), a momentum oscillator that identifies when a stock is overbought or oversold. RSI is based on an index between 0 and 100. When the calculated RSI value trends above 70, the stock is overbought and is likely to decline; and when it moves below 30, the stock is oversold.

In addition to these features built into all the charts, the following identifies price movement in the form of traditional technical signals, candlesticks, and movement near or at resistance and support. No one signals can predict consistently when to enter or exit a position, but in combination, these indicators confirm one another.

---

[1] Standard deviation is a statistical calculation for Bollinger Bands with six steps: (1) figure the simple average of the last 20 sessions; (2) find the deviation of this average, which is equal to the closing price minus the average; (3) find the square of each session's deviation; (4) add the squared deviations; (5) divide the total of these squared deviations by the number of periods to find the average of the deviation; and (6) find the square root of the average to identify standard deviation.

The charts are busy with a lot of detail. However, by tracking each highlighted indicator, you will get a good idea of how the charting process works and how reversals are spotted.

AT&T (T)

The three-month chart of T reveals numerous important technical signals. These signals are shown in Figure 4.1.

The following noteworthy signals are seen on the chart:

1. *Four candlestick reversal signals.* Marked on the chart are bearish meeting lines, confirmed a week later by a bearish engulfing; and a bullish harami confirmed immediately by a three identical white soldiers signal. The combination of reversal and confirmation adds strength to indicated reversals.

2. *Prices outside the outer bands.* It is unusual for prices to violate the two standard deviations represented by the outer Bollinger Bands. When this occurs, an immediate retracement back into range should

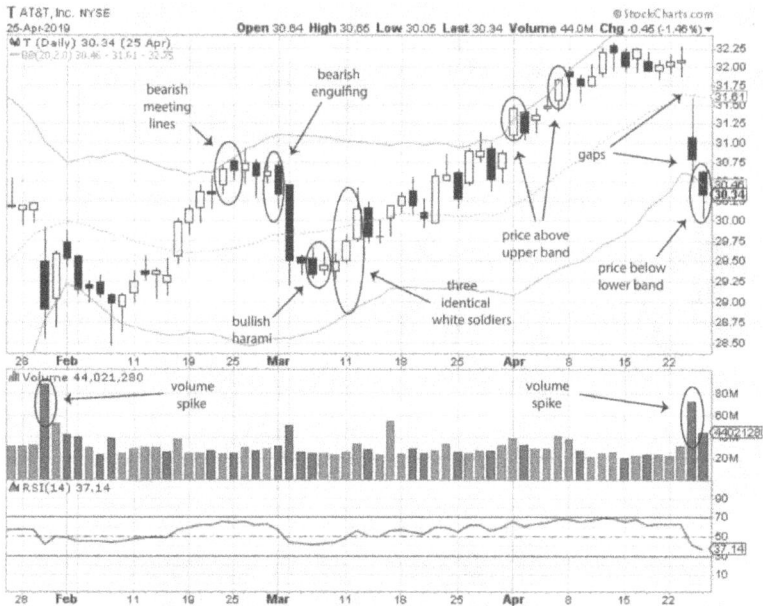

Figure 4.1 AT&T, three-month chart

Source: Chart coutesy of StockCharts.com

be expected. In this case, the bullish trend continues but the two band violations are connected within a single day. At the end of the chart, recurring gaps took price to close below the lower band. Price retraced higher on the following day (data not shown).

3. *Gaps.* Piece gaps are common, but large price gaps are rare, notably as they recur in a short time span. These cases involved two consecutive gaps, the first one covering nearly two full points.

4. *Volume spikes.* Among the strongest reversals is the volume spike, but it matters where the spike is seen. On this chart, two significant spikes are identified. The first occurs at the bottom of a downtrend, anticipating the strong upward reversal two weeks later. The second occurred at the end of the chart, where recurring gaps moved price below the lower band.

Southern Co. (SO)

This company's stock price has not been as volatile as some, and in fact showed a bullish trend for the first two months. Significant price signals

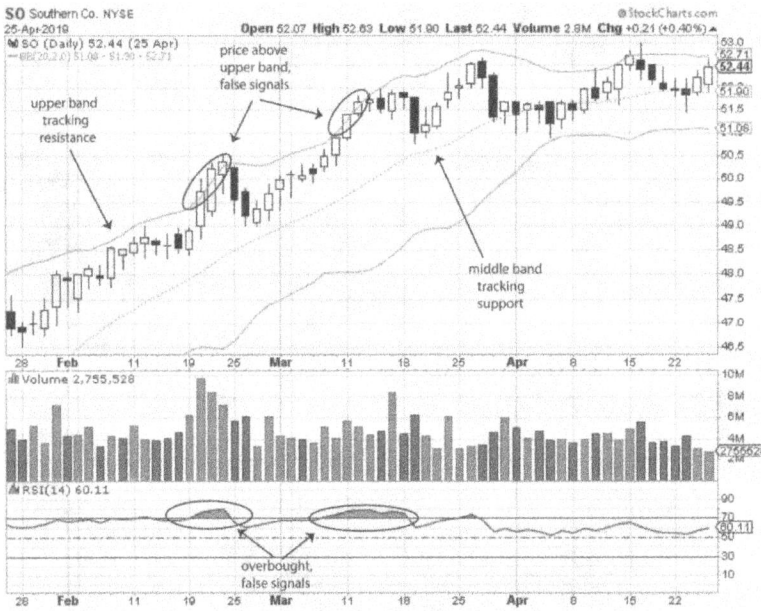

Figure 4.2 Southern Co., three-month chart

Source: Chart coutesy of StockCharts.com

were accompanied by momentum; however, these were good examples of false signals, as shown in Figure 4.2.

1. *Resistance and support tracking.* Bollinger Bands provides exceptional dynamic tracking of resistance and support during long-term trends. On this chart, the upper band tracked rising resistance, and the middle band tracked rising support.
2. *Price above upper band.* Two separate moves of price above the upper band appeared as bullish breakout at first glance, but both were false signals. Price retreated into range immediately.
3. *Overbought signals in RSI.* Although RSI is normally a reliable momentum oscillator, in this case the two instances of overbought confirmed the price moves but were false signals. In each case, momentum levels returned to mid-levels, and price continued rising.

Altria (MO)

This is a chart with low activity and a lack of strong signals, as shown in Figure 4.3.

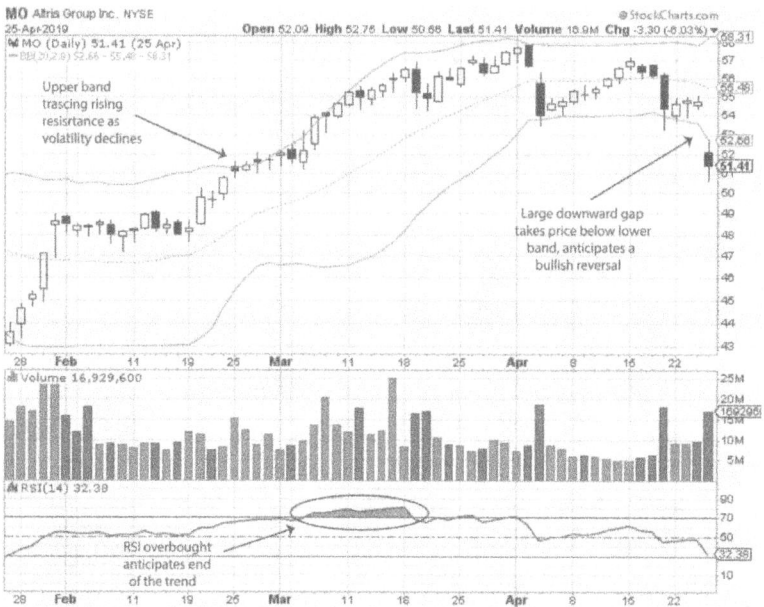

Figure 4.3 MO, three-month chart

Source: Chart coutesy of StockCharts.com

1. *Upper band tracking rising resistance.* While volatility was high, considerable space was seen between middle and outer bands. As volatility declined, the upper band tracked rising resistance closely.

2. *Momentum anticipated an end to the trend.* RSI moved into overbought and remained there for an unusually long time, about two weeks. As RSI retreated into midrange, it marked the end of the bullish trend.

3. *Large downward gap anticipated a bullish reversal.* Big gaps are exceptions, especially when they move price outside of the Bollinger Band range. At the end of the chart, the large gap anticipated a bullish reversal, which occurred next (data not shown).

For conservative traders, the analysis of chart patterns improves the timing for all entry and exit from trades. However, even with this worthwhile information, you need to continuously manage profits and losses and keep a conservative theme in your portfolio. The next chapter explains how this is accomplished.

Class questions for discussion and/or mini-case studies

Multiple choice

1. Fundamentally sound companies are defined in part as those with:
   a. Significant net profits in the most recent fiscal year.
   b. Growing revenue and earnings over the past 10 years.
   c. Higher than average dividends without regard to other signals.
   d. Decreasing revenues but increasing net profits.
2. A reversal should be acted upon when:
   a. Chart signals are strong, and confirmation is also strong.
   b. Only one reversal is located, whether confirmation is also found or not.
   c. Fundamentals are strong at the same time.
   d. The reversal is found only in the price trend.
3. Diversifying in trades may consist of:
   a. Spreading investment dollars among all stocks in the same industry.
   b. Picking the lowest-priced stocks only to get more variety.

    c. Equal numbers of calls and puts on the same stock.

    d. Using about the same dollar value for each trade and using several
       stocks.

Discussion:

Get updated charts for the three stocks in the mode, portfolio (T, SO, and
MO) and identify key reversal and confirmation signals for each, as well
as other important and noteworthy elements found on each chart.

CHAPTER 5

Managing Profits and Losses

The conservative risk profile discourages short-term decisions, and speculation is contrary to a safe and sensible investing philosophy. A buy–hold–sell technique is buying well-selected, high-quality stocks, hold for the long term, and sell only when the fundamentals change. This smart investing approach does not preclude protecting profits when price levels become volatile. You do not want to begin as a conservative and end up as a speculator. However, there are ways to take profits without selling stock and without increasing market risks. In some instances, taking market risks makes sense, even though it is not always a wise move.

Begin by making distinctions between various investor profiles. A conservative investor is interested in preserving capital and, as a result, wants to avoid risks. In stock market terms, risk usually refers to volatility (technical risk) or weak financial position (fundamental risk). A moderate investor is willing to assume somewhat greater risks if the potential for higher profits is present as well. A speculator or aggressive investor seeks the highest possible returns—often short term—and is willing to accept the highest levels of risk.

The label you use to define yourself is likely to be challenged when you come to the question of when and how to take profits. Recalling that profit-taking normally involves selling stock, it is contrary to your conservative profile to dispose of stock you would rather keep. But when you involve options, your choices expand significantly. Option strategies provide methods for protecting paper profits as they exist today, making smart moves when market conditions change and taking profits without needing to sell stock.

Your Conservative Dilemma

A conservative policy is intended to protect your investments from loss. By selecting high-quality companies, you eliminate the volatility that threatens your portfolio's value, and you set the goal of building equity over many years. Even so, you must contend with ever-changing market conditions and the prospect of needing to modify your mix of stocks. The most readily available information is short term by nature, so you must continually ensure that your portfolio-based buy–hold–sell decisions are made using *valid* information.

Reacting to short-term indicators and trends is human nature, but it can adversely affect the timing of decisions in your conservative portfolio. The conflict between short-term market trends and your long-term mindset is efficiently managed with options. Used in the proper context for managing price volatility and not as a primary and speculative change in policy, options help smooth out the price volatility that characterizes the market while protecting profits.

Deciding How to Establish Your Policies

If you have observed trends over time, you know that the price gyrations occurring this week and this month have a short-term aspect and a long-term aspect. You are keenly aware of what occurs from one day to the next, and you see daily reactions to political and business news, to earnings surprises, to rumors of economic trends, and to an unending number of other reasons for prices to rise or fall. But in the long-term context, short-term price changes and the daily reasons for price volatility really have nothing to do with long-term value. It is most logical to invest in high-quality stocks, monitor the fundamentals, and ignore short-term trends altogether.

Even the most ardent fundamental investor may not want to take this approach exclusively. Profit-taking is tempting. There is a way to take profits without selling stock. Some forms of trading can be made with little or no market risk. In Chapter 6, you see how covered call writing using appreciated stock achieves this end.

Selling stock when its price demonstrates short-term change is usually contrary to your conservative strategy. However, rapid price movement may also signal a change in the company attributes. Using any strategy does not necessarily contradict your conservative rule.

Managing Profits with Options

Investors often ignore the real problem of "managing" profits. (It may seem odd to refer to the "management" of profits because the usual thinking is you either sell to take profits or leave them intact; but, in fact, management is precisely what you want to do, even when your primary emphasis is on long-term growth.)

The traditional suggestion to buy long-term stocks and ignore short-term volatility is generally good advice. But ironically, it may also be irresponsible to simply leave it as such. Your ongoing portfolio management involves many chores, mostly centered on monitoring fundamental indicators. If corporate strength, competitive position, dividend payments, earnings trends, capitalization, and other fundamentals change, you may decide to sell shares and redirect your capital elsewhere. This is basic and sensible.

Basing Decisions on the Fundamentals

Conservative portfolio management is based on the fundamentals. Short-term price volatility—a technical indicator—can also be an early warning of emerging changes in the fundamentals. If volatility is a symptom of other problems—notably, of changes in fundamental strength—watching prices carefully is sensible. It is not reliable, however; most market theories agree that short-term movement cannot be used as a predictive tool. When prices are volatile, this may serve as a signal seeking confirmation that the fundamentals still work.

If price volatility is related to a serious decline in fundamental strength, it helps identify a change far earlier than traditional methods. Price volatility does not consistently provide early signals; much of the short-term volatility represents marketwide short-term trends, overreaction to news and events, or buying and selling trends among institutional investors who have little or nothing to do with the stock's long-term growth potential.

The traditional advice given to conservative investors wanting to ensure safety is to diversify their portfolios. Although diversification is a sensible idea, it does nothing to contend with short-term price volatility. Even with the best diversification, you still experience price surges and declines; you still want to take profits or buy more stock at depressed prices; and you must resist the temptation to react to short-term trends for the wrong reasons. Diversification protects you against specific risks, but it does nothing to ensure that you will not have to live through price volatility.

Yet another expansion of the diversified portfolio is to adopt a model for *asset allocation*. Under this variation, you "allocate" portions of your capital in different markets: stocks, mutual funds, real estate, cash reserves, precious metals, and so on. Asset allocation makes sense for the same reasons that diversification does, but it does not protect your portfolio from short-term volatility.

The Reality of Risk

You cannot avoid all forms of risk. But you can protect yourself. The two methods of protecting profits with options are buying puts and selling covered calls. Each of the attributes of these strategies is worth comparing. Table 5.1 summarizes features of the long put and the short call.

The decision to use long puts or short calls rests with your long-term opinions about long or short positions. If you view long puts as strictly working to provide insurance, it is conservative to protect profits without risking stock positions. In comparison, covered call writing presents the

Table 5.1 Long put and short call features

Buying puts	Selling calls
This provides a form of insurance on long stock holdings	This sets up a contingent sale in the event of exercise
Stock price decline sees decreased put premium value	Stock price decline is offset by reduced call premium value
Price offset is unlimited as long as the put remains open	Price offset is limited to premium received
A trader pays to acquire the put	A trader is paid for selling the call
Time value decline may offset ITM gains	Time value decline is profitable in the short position

possibility of exercise in exchange for money flowing in rather than out and for providing a reduction in your basis, thus programmed higher profits in the event of exercise. This downside protection makes short calls more attractive in most respects. However, if you view covered calls as inappropriate because you do not want to have shares called away, the long put may be the best method for protecting your profits.

Overcoming the Profit-Taking Problem

The debate about whether it is conservative to use options depends on the timing and motives behind your decision. Buying options to speculate is inconsistent with your conservative goals.

You need to identify the lowest likely price level for the stock. Support is a technical term, of course, and most conservative investors do not use support and resistance as decision-making tools. An understanding of the support level within your conservative risk profile helps you coordinate option strategies that enable profit-taking without needing to sell stock.

Realizing Profits Without Selling Stock

As a conservative investor, you do not want to make profits just because the current price of stock is higher than your basis; it would certainly be desirable to realize profits without selling stock. A few guidelines help clarify this dilemma:

1. It is appropriate to use long puts to protect existing portfolio positions. The long put, as insurance, represents a limited risk and ensures that current profitable price levels are protected.

2. It is appropriate to use long calls only as a form of contingent purchase, when long-term options (LEAPS) are available and when the purpose is to reserve the possibility of exercising those calls to purchase shares of stock. (See Chapter 9 for more in-depth discussions.)

3. Long calls are useful if prices of stocks you currently own have fallen rapidly due to marketwide price declines; this presents a buying opportunity, but you may be unwilling to purchase additional shares as a means of exploiting the temporary condition. Calls can be exer-

cised to acquire additional shares to reduce your overall basis in the stock.

4. Short puts are useful as a form of contingent purchase (in which you would have shares put to you at the strike price when exercised), but only when you would be pleased to purchase shares at the net price (strike price reduced by put premium you receive). Support level is by no means an absolute value. You may employ fundamental tests to find what you consider the stock's support level.

5. You can use short puts in place of long calls when prices of stock you own have declined and you expect near-term prices to rise. This assumes you are willing to acquire shares at the strike if the put is exercised.

When is the decision to employ options speculative, and when is it a valid conservative strategy? One consideration is whether you already have a position in the stock. If your purpose in using options is to protect profits, exploit price swings, or average down your cost of stock, your conservative standards are compatible with using options in a variety of ways. If you use options to time market price movement in stocks you do not own, it is only appropriate for contingent purchase strategies, qualified by the preceding conditions. Otherwise, using options just as a means for profiting in stocks you do not own is speculative.

When a Rescue Strategy Is Appropriate

This rescue strategy is any decision designed to recover from a loss in one position, by offsetting that loss with a new position. This is appropriate only when (a) fundamental strength continues to qualify the stock as a long-term growth investment; (b) you have capital available to purchase more shares or to trade options; and (c) you are willing to invest in a single stock, either through equity or options. The drop in price levels could be a problem; however, if the fundamental value of stock has not changed and you want to continue to hold shares, a rescue strategy helps reduce basis *and* offset a past loss.

Another rescue strategy following the acquisition of stock through exercised short puts is to revert to a covered call strategy. The outcome of this strategy is positive from all angles:

- You buy more shares, but your basis is reduced to the average between original shares and newly acquired shares.
- You earn a premium from writing short puts and short calls, all of which is yours to keep.
- You have a capital gain on the shares acquired and then called away.
- You come out of the series of transactions with the original number of shares after exercise, which is unencumbered and can be held for long-term growth (but at a lower basis), or to provide coverage for additional short call positions.

If puts are not exercised, you could wait for expiration or close prior to expiration at a profit. Once they are expired or closed, you can write more short puts. However, if the price of stock rebounded during the life of the puts, you would not want to repeat the short put strategy, at least not at the same strike. If the puts' value declines, you can enter a closing purchase transaction. The net difference between your original sale and later purchase is profitable.

The greatest problem with strategies like this is the complexity of the transaction. To execute a series of trades involving short puts and short calls, changes in basis, and the number of shares owned, some conservative investors are understandably discouraged. It requires confidence and skill to deal with the details. Considering that the purpose of the transaction is to manage a decline in market value and to turn it into a profitable position, it is worth overcoming the initial learning curve. However, you should also ensure that before you enter the short positions, you fully understand the potential consequences, as well as the benefits, of every possible outcome.

Taxes and Profits

The strategies you employ to either protect paper profits or minimize paper losses may be profitable or not, depending on your tax status. If a profitable or breakeven situation is calculated on a pretax basis, it may end up at a net loss after tax liabilities are calculated.

To assess strategic decisions with tax liabilities in mind, include the following points in your analysis:

- **Carryover loss status.** As a planning tool, carryover losses are easily forgotten or ignored. If your carryover loss is substantial, you may absorb that loss by taking gains this year that you might not have taken otherwise. As inconvenient as carryover losses are, they provide a planning opportunity.

    A sale of stock should occur without use of options. Upon sale, wait 31 days before repurchasing stock to avoid the wash sale rule, or sell ITM puts at the strike price close to your sale price.

- **Your true effective tax rate.** When you calculate the tax effect of capital gains on stock or options, be sure to include both federal and state taxes. Your "true" effective rate is the combined rate of both. The effective rate is the percentage of tax on any earnings reported under your tax bracket, where Federal and state effective tax rates must be added together.

- **The timing of your profits and losses.** Traditional tax planning involves preplanned timing of taxable gains and, equally important, of tax losses. You can time your profits and losses based on your tax status this year. However, your priority in timing of transactions should be set first on your conservative goals. Only when it makes no difference should the tax questions come into play.

- **Offsetting profits and losses in the same year.** One of the most effective planning devices is to simply match profits against current-year losses. The outcome has little or no net change on your effective tax rate. If your rate is close to the point where additional income would push your taxes into the next bracket, preplanning makes sense. If you intend to take profits, it may also be smart to dispose the underperforming stock. You gain two advantages by coordinating the timing of these transactions. First, you shelter gains by offsetting them with investment losses. Second, you dispose of stocks that have not performed as you hoped.

- **Unintended tax consequences.** The tax rules for options-related transactions are complex. For many individuals, the tax rules are too complicated even without options, so many people who simply buy and sell stocks, mutual funds, and real estate hire tax experts to help them comply with the law. When you add options to the mix, the complexity makes professional help more important than ever. Consult with your expert before making trades so that you understand the rules and know beforehand which types of trades can cause significant loss of tax advantage.

Options Used for Riding Out Volatility

Everyone must contend with short-term price volatility. As a conservative investor, you focus on fundamental attributes of the company and use short-term indicators only to test your ongoing assumptions. If those assumptions change, your hold strategy may become a sell. However, if you intend to continue holding stock, options can be valuable in riding out short-term volatility as an alternative to profit-taking in the traditional manner. With options, you can minimize short-term losses and even take profits while continuing to own shares of stock.

In the next chapter, the intriguing possibilities of the covered call strategy, including the special tax rules that apply to short options strategies, are explored in depth.

Class questions for discussion and/or mini-case studies

1. The "buy and hold" strategy involves:
   a. Buying stock and holding options on those stocks.
   b. Buying options only and holding until expiration.
   c. Buying and holding stock for a very short term.
   d. Buying stock for the long term and not selling.

2. Price volatility demonstrates that:

   a. Diversification does not solve short-term risk-related problems.

   b. Market risks make stocks inappropriate in a conservative portfolio.

   c. A robust market involves uncertainty without exception.

   d. Relying on fundamental trends is a more sensible way to trade.

3. You can realize profits without selling shares of stock by:

   a. Selling and immediately rebuying the same shares.

   b. Selling and waiting for retracement, and then repurchasing shares.

   c. Trading short or long options and taking profits through options rather than stock.

   d. Executing a series of wash sales to time extreme price moves.

Discussion

Locate the stock chart of a company whose price per share has declined during recent activity. Explain at least two recovery strategies that can be utilized in this situation.

CHAPTER 6

Options as Cash Generators

The covered call is among the most attractive of conservative option strategies. It provides an impressive rate of return when properly structured, and it does not increase the most common forms of risk. In fact, market risk—your exposure to lost value in your stock—is reduced with the covered call strategy.

In this chapter, the conservative possibilities of covered calls are explained, starting with the underlying premise necessary to succeed with this strategy. Various outcome scenarios help you form realistic judgments about whether the covered call strategy makes sense.

The Covered Call Concept

No strategy is completely risk-free, not even owning stock in well-managed, strongly capitalized companies. But in the case of a covered call, you seek to enhance profits without incurring added market risk, and the advantage is both practical and inevitable. For many investors, the lost opportunity risk is worth the additional income that covered call strategies generate. (Lost opportunity risk is discussed later in this chapter.)

A covered call strategy has two elements. First is the ownership of 100 shares of stock for each option to be covered; second is the short position in the call option. If you own 100 shares, you sell one call to achieve the one-to-one "covered" status. The call grants the right to the buyer on the other side of the transaction to buy your 100 shares (to call them away) at the set strike price at any time from the date of sale until expiration. If the current price of stock is below the strike price, the call will not be exercised.

Who Makes the Decision?

When you enter a covered call position, you sell the call against stock you own. This means you give the right to exercise to the buyer, and that decision is entirely in the buyer's hands. You can keep the cash you receive upon selling the short call, whether the call is exercised, closed, or simply expires. You also continue to receive dividends during the period you are short on the call. The big question comes down to this: Is it worthwhile to risk having 100 shares of stock called away if the stock's price moves above the call's strike?

The covered calls produce instant cash. You are paid for selling the call. For example, if you can achieve an immediate 10 percent return on your stock by selling a call, is it worthwhile? The answer, of course, depends on your original purchase prices versus today's stock value as well as the call's strike.

The disadvantage to selling covered calls is that, first, you tie up 100 shares for each call sold, and you cannot escape from the covered position without closing out that short call. Second, your maximum profit is always limited to the premium received for the call.

You should close the position under one of two circumstances. First, if the value of the short call has declined since the position was opened, you can pay the current price and close at a profit. Second, you may close if the value of stock has moved upward beyond the strike. In this situation, you face the possibility of exercise, which can happen at any time when the call is in the money. When the stock's price moves above the strike, the net premium value of the short call may be lower than it was when you sold it. This is true because the call's time value declines as the exercise date draws near. In this situation, it is prudent to buy and avoid exercise while still realizing a net gain on the call transaction. Incidentally, once you close out the covered call position, you are free to repeat the trade, using calls with higher strike prices and later expiration dates.

If the stock's price moves above strike price so that your short call is ITM, the call's value may also have increased. You can still avoid exercise without taking a net loss using a technique called rolling (replacement of one call with another). This strategy is explained in detail later in this chapter.

Examples: Three Stocks and Covered Calls

To illustrate how the basic covered call strategy works, examine the three companies in the model portfolio, sharing three common attributes:

1. Both listed options and LEAPS are available on the stocks.
2. All these stocks are assumed to have current market value above the original basis.
3. All stocks show current moderate price volatility levels.

These stocks' basic attributes are summarized in Table 6.1.

Table 6.1 Sample stocks for covered calls

Name of company	Symbol	Current Price ($)*	Dividend Yield (%)
AT&T	T	30.34	6.64
Southern Co.	SO	52.44	4.66
Altria	MO	51.41	5.95

*As of April 25, 2019. Source: Charles Schwab & Co.

The next step is to analyze a series of options in comparative form. If you compare options with different expiration terms, you should annualize those returns. A summary of call option values expiring in 57 days is shown in Table 6.2.

Table 6.2 Covered call premium, 57 days to expiration

Name of company	Symbol	Current Price ($)*	57-day strike	Call bid premium	Yield (%)**
AT&T	T	30.34	30.50	1.02	3.34
Southern Co.	SO	52.44	52.50	0.94	1.79
Altria	MO	51,41	52.50	1.29	2.46

* As of April 25, 2019. Source: Charles Schwab & Co.
** Premium divided by strike.

This table shows a comparative yield. Time to expiration is identical for all three companies; and the strike selected is closest to the current price of stock.

Smart Conservative Ground Rules

All strategies have positive and negative aspects. The covered call strategy is conservative if you understand the transaction's specific attributes and that you are sure the numbers work in your favor. Following are a few basic ground rules as you proceed through the analysis to ensure a truly conservative application of the covered call strategy:

- **Your original purchase price must justify the strategy.** The most conservative use of covered calls exists when you own stock that has appreciated in value. The lower your basis in comparison with today's market value of stock, the more flexibility you have in devising a conservative options strategy.

- **The premium value you receive must provide enough yield to justify the covered call exposure.** If you plan to use your stock as cover for a short option position, you must be able to justify it in terms of profit levels. If you own shares of many different stocks, you will naturally seek out those option positions that yield the best returns.

- **You are willing to accept exercise as one of the possible outcomes.** In every covered call position, you must accept the possibility that your 100 shares of stock will be called away. If you do not want exercise under any circumstances, you should not write covered calls.

- **The primary risk to the covered call strategy is possible loss of future market gains if stock prices exceed the call's strike price.** This lost opportunity risk should be understood before you enter any covered call strategy.

- **The covered call strategy commits capital invested in stock for as long as the short call remains open.** Since a conservative strategy requires that your long stock position is maintained as an offset to the short call, your shares are committed until the short position is closed. You escape this commitment when you buy to close the call, when the call is exercised, or when the call expires.

- **Most important of all, your primary portfolio strategy must remain the same, seeking long-term investment in the stock of properly selected companies, not in selecting stocks based only on potential covered call returns.** One danger in using options to enhance profits is that it could change your entire investment strategy. As a conservative investor, your first rule should be that, no matter what, the proper selection of companies based on fundamental strength and growth prospects must remain the primary means of stock selection and the primary deciding factor for any decision to buy, hold, or sell shares.

A Conservative Approach

Proceeding from the ground rules for covered call writing, the next step is to determine exactly what makes elements of the strategy advantageous. As a conservative investor, what are the primary attributes you need to enter a profitable conservative strategy? There are three: appreciated value in the stock, time and extrinsic value premium, and downside protection.

Element 1: Appreciated Value in the Stock

If the current value is higher than your basis, you have great profit flexibility in entering a covered call strategy. In other words, with those paper profits, you can build in a greater certainty of profits.

Example: Covered Calls without Substantial Appreciated Value in the Stock
You purchased 1,400 shares of AT&T stock at $28 per share; today, shares are worth $30.34. You sell 14 of the 85-day 30-strike call and receive a premium of 114, or $1,596 for 14 contracts (assuming a typical trading fee of $15, assume the net received was $1,581). If exercised, total return on stock and option transactions (without adjusting for annualization or taxes) would be:

Capital gain = 30 strike, 1,400 shares, $42,476 less $28 per share basis
= $39,200
Net capital gain = $3,276

Capital gain yield = $3,276 ÷ $39,200 = 8.36% (before annualizing)

Option premium = $1,581

Option return (premium divided by strike) = $1,581 ÷ $30,000 = 5.27%

To accurately annualize the overall yield, option outcome should be separated from capital gains on stock. Why? Based on both holding period and dollar value of the gain, side-by-side comparisons will be distorted. In this example, there are two separate yields, one each from capital gains and options. This is even further complicated by the holding period of stock and by the timing of exercise of the covered call. Finally, the number of quarterly dividends earning during the holding period make it even more difficult to arrive at a valid annualized return, especially when comparing one outcome to another.

Element 2: Time and Extrinsic Value Premium

The key to successful covered call writing is in the time value premium. If the call is ATM or OTM, there is no intrinsic value. Time works for the seller and against the buyer. Buying options can be highly speculative because the buyer must hope not only that the stock rises enough to create intrinsic value prior to expiration but also that the growth in price rises far enough to offset lost time value. Since time value evaporates as expiration approaches, it is difficult to achieve.

Time and extrinsic values from the seller's point of view are the advantage. Knowing that time value declines no matter how the stock's price moves by expiration, the time value premium is a cushion, made even more generous when extrinsic value is high.

Element 3: Downside Protection

Every investor whose stock has appreciated in value worries about losing paper profits, so profit-taking is more likely as paper profits increase. Well-disciplined conservative strategy tells you that you should not give in to the temptation to speculate on short-term price movements, that is, by taking profits. However, as the adage tells you, "Wall Street climbs a wall of worry."

Selling covered calls against appreciated stocks is one way to offset your personal wall of worry. The premium you receive from selling covered calls is, in a sense, a way of taking profits without giving up ownership of shares. Those profits are yours to keep in the event of expiration or exercise, and if you close the position by buying the short call the difference between sell and buy price represents profit or loss.

The net premium you earn from selling calls can be viewed in another way: as downside protection. Viewing covered calls in this way, you achieve a broader range of profit margin, meaning more downside protection. The more premium you receive from selling calls over time, the greater your downside protection.

Tax Ramifications of Covered Calls

Calculating returns without figuring out the after-tax outcome is not realistic. Not only must you consider a tax liability, you need to be aware that the tax rules can drastically affect your tax rate on capital gains. The current rules for federal taxes on option trades are more complex than for most forms of investing. For conservative investors, a crucial point to remember is that selling OTM calls is the least complicated strategy for two reasons. First, the entire premium consists of time and extrinsic values. Second, the tax rules are simple if you restrict your trades to OTM positions, so there is no effect on the calculation of short-term or long-term capital gains holding periods. However, once you sell an ITM call, the whole question becomes much more complicated. Here is a rundown of the tax rules governing options:

- **Rules for option buyers.** If you buy options, the profit or loss can either be long term or short term depending on how long you own the long option. The net amount is reported on federal tax Schedule D (Capital Gains and Losses) in the year of sale. If the transaction is completed within one year or less, it is taxed as a short-term capital gain or loss. If the total holding period was longer than one year, it is treated as a long-term gain or loss.
- **Rules for option sellers.** The rules for option sellers are different than for other types of investments. The payment

you receive at the time of sale is not taxed at that point.
The tax "event" occurs when the position is closed, expired,
or exercised. If you sell an option in one year and it is
closed in the next, the tax is not calculated until the latter
year.

One important exception to the general rule governing short-term
and long-term tax rates is that if you keep a short call until expiration, it
is treated as a short-term gain or loss, no matter how long the position
was open. For example, you may sell a covered LEAPS call that does not
expire for 30 months. Upon expiration, the gain is considered short term.
If you close out the position with a buy order prior to expiration, it is
treated as short term if it was open for one year or less or as long term if
the holding period was open more than a year.

If the call is exercised and your stock is called away, the gain is fig-
ured including the premium you received from sale of the call and the
gain on stock. For example, if your capital gain was $2,400 and you
received $830 for the option, all the gain—$3,230—is treated in the
same manner. This treatment depends on the holding period of the
stock and whether the call is defined under IRS rules as a "qualified"
covered call.

Nonqualified covered calls affect the calculation of the long-term
gain holding period. If the option you sell is ATM or OTM, the holding
period for your stock is not affected or stopped. If the call is ITM and
it meets the definition of qualified, the holding period is not changed.
If the call is nonqualified, however, the holding period counting toward
long-term gain treatment is done away with and, for the purposes of
calculating gain, the time limit begins anew once the call position has
been closed.

Example: You own stock currently valued at $75 per share. You sell
a covered call ITM (below the current value of the stock). In this case,
the status of long-term or short-term gain is determined by the rules for
qualification for the call. If the call is defined as unqualified, the holding
period of stock is suspended and the call position is open. Your stock's
holding period is eliminated entirely and starts over once the call is closed.
The time limit stops running if the call remains open.

Six Levels of Separation (of Your Money) for Taxes

The following applies only to ITM covered calls. There are six separate levels of calculation:

1. The previous day's closing stock price is $25 or less, and the option has more than 30 days to go until expiration.
2. The previous day's closing stock price is between $25.01 and $60.00, and the option has more than 30 days until expiration.
3. The previous day's closing stock price is between $60.01 and $150, and the option expires in 31 to 90 days.
4. The previous day's closing stock price is between $60.01 and $150, and the option expires beyond 90 days.
5. The previous day's closing stock price is greater than $150 per share, and the option will expire between 31 and 90 days.
6. The previous day's closing stock price is greater than $150 per share, and the option expires beyond 90 days.

The conservative investor should seek OTM covered calls exclusively. This simplifies the tax calculations and conforms to the commonsense standards defining a conservative strategy. One exception to this general rule is if you have large carryover losses, you may not be concerned with taxation of current-year capital gains. Since annual capital losses are limited to $3,000 maximum, a large carryover loss may be used to absorb current-year gains. So, even if you lose long-term capital gains status for exercised stock, this large carryover loss presents a planning advantage; you can engage in ITM covered call writing without worrying about long-term or short-term restrictions.

Rolling Forward and Up: Exercise Avoidance

You can avoid the complexities of the tax rules by utilizing only OTM covered calls. For conservative investors, this makes sense even without considering how federal taxes affect the strategy. It affects planning if you intend to create a forced sale using deep ITM calls ("deep" means more than 5 points below strike price). Under the definitions in the tax rules, it would convert all stock sales to short term because the options would be nonqualified.

Rather than seeking forced exercise, most conservative investors prefer to keep ownership of the stock and use options to maximize short-term income, hopefully in a repetitive fashion. Exercise avoidance is a far more attractive strategy for most people.

Since covered call writers must accept the possibility of exercise, why avoid it? Although exercise is a possibility, it is often preferable to keep well-selected stocks in the portfolio and to take steps to (a) avoid having it called away, (b) be able to continue writing subsequent calls, and (c) in the event of exercise, maximize income from the transaction. All this requires employing a rolling technique.

Types of Rolls

In a roll, you buy to close a current open position while you sell to open a subsequent position that has one of three possible attributes:

1. **A roll forward.** The new covered call expires later than the old covered call but at the same strike price. Caution: If the stock price moves above this strike price, you risk converting your OTM covered call into an ITM call, so the tax picture of stock profits changes.
2. **A roll up.** The new covered call expires at the same time but at a higher strike price. With this strategy, expiration remains the same, but you "buy" another 5 points of profit in the event of exercise. The difference of 5 points may be only 2 or 3 points of net cost, so if you expect the stock's price to continue rising, losing a few points in the exchange of one option for another is not negative in every instance. The net difference in buying out of the current position and opening the new one is 2 points, but you gain 5 points in the higher strike price, while converting your ITM short call to a new, OTM short call.
3. **A roll forward and up.** The new covered call expires later than the old covered call and at a higher strike price. This is the most desirable rolling method. It is possible to execute a forward-and-up roll while still producing a net credit. It means more premium income as well

as a higher potential exercise price. By avoiding exercise, you gain more net income, and you also gain 5 points in strike.

The Exercise Acceptance Strategy

A final idea is the exercise acceptance strategy. Most conservative investors are content to keep their long-term stocks and to use well-selected OTM calls to create additional profits along with downside protection. However, what if you would be happy to see your call exercised?

Selling covered calls is a profitable alternative to simply owning stock. You can also force exercise by intentionally writing ITM calls. However, since this ensures the loss of long-term status of capital gains when exercise occurs, the strategy must be studied on an after-tax basis. When you have a large carryover loss from previous years, it could be an effective way to create large option premium gains and absorb unused carryover. Your annual net loss deduction is limited to $3,000, but if you have a $30,000 carryover it would take 10 years to use it up without future offsetting capital gains. It is desirable to absorb that loss as soon as possible; in this case, creating a large gain in stock and options by writing deep ITM covered calls (virtually ensuring exercise) would be beneficial because the loss of long-term status is sheltered by the carryover loss.

Limiting Yourself to Conservative Strategies

You probably consider covered calls a conservative strategy because no increased market risk is involved. The alternative, simply owning shares of stock, has an inherent market risk, and discounting the basis by generating call premium reduces the basis in stock which also lowers the net market risk. Covered call writing involves lost opportunity risk; in reviewing likely scenarios for several stocks, you know that such lost opportunities occur in a minority of cases, while consistent high returns from covered calls are certain.

In the next chapter, interesting ways to use options as an alternative to the purchase of shares of stock are explored. The iron butterfly is a hedging strategy, and this can be expanded to create a matrix of hedging over three or more expiration dates.

Class questions for discussion and/or mini-case studies

1. The covered call contains two elements:
   a. A short call and a long put.
   b. A long call and a short put.
   c. A call and a put, both short.
   d. A short call matched to 100 shares of stock.
2. Common attributes of viable covered call candidates include:
   a. Availability of options on the underlying.
   b. Current market value of the underlying above net basis.
   c. Moderate price volatility.
   d. All of the above.
3. Rolling usually refers to the action of closing a covered call and replacing it with:
   a. A covered put.
   b. A later-expiring short call below the strike of the original call.
   c. A later-expiring call at the same strike or a higher strike.

Discussion

Identify a stock chart appropriate for writing covered calls. Calculate the net basis in stock if shares were purchased today and a covered call written; analyze the potential recovery strategy if share price declined.

CHAPTER 7

The 1-2-3 Iron Butterfly

The butterfly spread is referred to as a "neutral" strategy combing a bull and bear spread with the same expiration date. It involves three different strikes and four options. The normal configuration involves two short options at the middle strike, and long options above and below. Either puts or calls can be used to create a butterfly spread.

The Iron Butterfly

The *iron butterfly* is an expansion of the butterfly, involving both calls and puts. For example, a long put is opened below the middle and a long call above, and the middle strike involves a short put and a short call.

For example, Altria closed on April 25, 2019 at $51.41 and you purchased 100 shares. On that date, an iron butterfly spread consisting of both calls and puts could have been opened with the following (adjusted by $5 for trading fee):

Long 29-day 50 put @ 0.96	=	101
Short 29-day 51 put @ 0.97	=	(92)
Short 29-day 51 call @ 1.54	=	(149)
Long 29-day 52.50 call @ 1.07	=	112
	Net credit	(28)

This position yields a net credit after trading drees. It has the potential to create limited maximum profits in exchange for minimum exposure to loss. Examining the outcome as of expiration at various underlying prices makes this point as summarized in Table 7.1.

This outcome reveals that if all positions were kept open to expiration, most price levels would realize a net loss of $72. Only at $51 per share would the minimal profit be realized. In practice, however, positions would not be held open until expiration, but closed as profits materialize.

Table 7.1 Altria iron butterfly

Strike*	May 3 (8 days)	Premium	May 24 (29 days)	Premium	Jun 21 (57 days)	Premium
50	1 put	0.38	2 puts	-1.30	3 puts	4.78
51	1 put	-0.48	2 puts	2.66	3 puts	-7.70**
52.50	1 call	-0.25	2 calls	2.20	3 calls	-3.80
53	1 call	0.28	2 calls	-1.14	3 calls	1.93***
Total		-0.07		2.42		-4.79
Net						-2.44

* Purchased options are increased to allow for fees, and are reflected at ask price. Sold options are decreased to allow for fees, and are reflected at bid price.

** June 51 put not available, premium reflects price of 7.70 for 52.50 puts.

*** June 53 call not available, premium reflects price of 1.93 for 55 calls.

A similar strategy is the condor, involving four strikes rather than three. Ideally, the underlying should be priced in the middle so that two options are opened below and two above. A short condor would consist of middle strike long and lower/upper strike short positions, just like the butterfly.

Many traders avoid butterflies and iron butterflies due to the limited profit potential. A conservative trader may be willing to accept limited profits in exchange for limited losses, but this limitation is difficult to overcome when trading costs are considered. Given the number of contracts (four) and trading costs at entry and at exit, there are a total of eight charges. A solution would be to open multiple contracts, or to expand the iron butterfly into a hedge with the idea of taking profits well before expiration. This is where the 1-2-3 iron butterfly comes into the picture.

The 1-2-3 Iron Butterfly Concept

Considering the commissions involved with a butterfly of any type, traders need to take one of two precautions. First, you must ensure that the net credit is adequate to cover trading costs while still producing potential

profits. Second, it makes sense in some instances to open multiple contracts to efficiently reduce the trading costs. Brokers charge a minimum
fee for the option trade and a very small additional fee for additional
options. For example, the minimum fee may be $5.75, plus 0.75 for each
option. The trading cost to enter and again to exit would be:

1. option $5.75 + 0.75 = $6.50
2. options $5.75 + 1.50 = $7.25
3. options $5.75 + 2.25 = $8.00
4. options $5.75 + 3.00 = $8.75

For one option the transaction cost is $6.50, but for four options the
average per option is reduced to $2.19 each ($8.75 ÷ 4).

The cost of trading is a considerable factor and cannot be overlooked.
For this reason alone, traders may want to involve multiple contracts
rather than single contracts. However, for purposes of comparison and
explanation, single-option examples are provided; however, these vary
considerably by broker and by the number of contracts.

The 1-2-3 iron butterfly consists of three separate iron butterflies, one
in each of the next three expiration periods. However, if the underlying
stock also pays a dividend, it is smart not to open positions during ex-dividend month to avoid the risk of early exercise. If the company pays a
dividend in October and January, the 1-2-3 iron butterfly may be set up
using November, December, and February.

The 1-2-3 iron butterfly—like the regular iron butterfly—is a combination of OTM and ATM strikes, or at least close to the money. It combines puts and calls. The 1-2-3 refers to two attributes. First is the user
of three expiration months. Second is the increased number of contracts
at each expiration. The first expiring month involves one option at each
strike, then two, and then three. Other increments can be used as well,
such as 2-4-6 or 3-6-9, for example.

Another distinguishing feature of the 1-2-3 iron butterfly is that the
middle month is a *reverse* iron butterfly, meaning the lower put and upper
call are both short, and the two ATM middle strikes are long. This is done
to set up a *hedge matrix*, the offset of profits in both calls and puts in three
months. This hedge matrix enables you to close options in one, two, or

three of the expiration months at a profit, no matter which direction the stock moves:

1. If the underlying price rises, long calls and short puts will become profitable in all three periods.
2. If the underlying price falls, long puts and short calls will become profitable in all three periods.
3. If the underlying price remains at or close to the initial entry price, all short options will lose time value and become profitable.

It does not guarantee that all positions will become profitable in all instances. This is where rolling forward is a smarty recovery strategy. Invariably, after closing most positions at a profit, a few positions remain open. These positions, whether long or short, can be closed at a loss and replaced with later-expiring long or short options. These leftover positions ("orphans") can be used to create a reconstituted 1-2-3 iron butterfly. This is necessary when the underlying has moved far above or below the strike range of the original options. These leftover positions are closed and replaced with new, later-expiring positions closer in range to the underlying price. Thus, the 1-2-3 iron butterfly can evolve with a stock whose price is moving, by carrying losses forward and adjusting the basis in new options.

For example, if your original long positions would lose $200 if closed today, but these are rolled forward and replaced with new options costing $300, the adjusted long basis is $500 ($200 loss carried forward plus $300 paid for the new long options). If the original short positions would lose $300 if closed today, but these are rolled forward and replaced with new options yielding $400, the net basis is $100 ($400 for selling new options minus $300 loss on the previous contracts).

Rolling forward works for both long and short sides. However, this also makes it more difficult to create a net profit later because of the adjustment in the net basis. This disadvantage is often offset by the faster profit accumulation because new strikes are closer to the current underlying price. The 1-2-3 is a complex set of transactions and should be used only by traders thoroughly familiar and experienced with options.

The Hedge Matrix and Collateral Requirements

The hedge matrix serves two purposes. First, it sets up a situation in which you can take profits, no matter what occurs in the underlying price. Second, it keeps collateral requirements at a minimum.

Collateral for uncovered short options is equal to 20 percent of the strike value minus premium received. For example, an uncovered 97.50 call or put must be accompanied by collateral of $1,950 ($9,750 * 20% = $1,950) minus option premium received. To calculate required margin for short positions, use the free margin calculator offered by the CBOE:

http://cboe.com/trading-tools/calculators/margin-calculator

You can also download a free Margin Manual to discover how margin requirements vary by type of option:

http://cboe.com/LearnCenter/pdf/margin2-00.pdf

Example of the Strategy

The 1-2-3 iron butterfly can be set up for any stock; however, it makes sense to also avoid the ex-dividend month to prevent early exercise. Any time a short call is ITM, you are at risk of early exercise in the ex-dividend month. This does not mean it will always happen, but it is a possibility. Having open short calls in the following month avoids this risk, because time value in the call will normally make early exercise impractical.

For a long call owner to justify early exercise, the combination of any capital gain plus dividend income must be greater than the cost of that call. Early exercise is most likely on the day before ex-dividend date. So even if a short call that is ITM is only marginally at risk, it may still get exercised if the long call holder would realize a capital gain. In that case, the gain plus dividend would create a very nice profit.

An example of the strategy follows, shown in Table 7.1, for Altria (MO). Ex-dividend months are January, April, July, and October. Based on the values on April 25, 2019, the following 1-2-3 iron butterfly could be opened, setting up an overall net credit.

Some explanations: Since not every option strike will be available at every expiration, this table has some adjusted strikes in use, in two instances. These occur in the last section, the June 21 options. The 51 put was not available, so three contracts were traded on the 52.50 put strike. The 53 call strike was not available, so three contracts were traded on the 55 call strike.

Although this changes the consistency of the 1-2-3 iron butterfly, the symmetry of the strategy is kept intact. The overall net credit yielded was 2.44 ($244). This would be the net realized value if all options expired worthless, which is unlikely because some positions will always be in the money. A more likely outcome would be to close positions when they become profitable and attempt to offset long and short positions.

The potential to offset one set of strikes against others with different expiration dates may cause a higher collateral requirement to go into effect. Any trader writing a 1-2-3 iron butterfly must be prepared to deposit additional funds in the event that short positions are left open for any one expiration without offsetting long positions.

The 1-2-3 iron butterfly and its hedge matrix can be applied to many different strategies that combine options to set up neutral outcomes or outcomes of net credits. By involving three separate expiration months, you can take the benefit of offsetting long and short positions to limit risk, while closing short and long positions together when profits materialize.

The next chapter explores another conservative strategy, the dividend collar. This is designed to eliminate market risk in the stock, while setting up option positions to earn dividends every month (instead of every quarter). This creates a double-digit dividend yield by moving in and out of positions in ex-dividend month.

Class questions for discussion and/or mini-case studies

1. The iron butterfly is a multipart strategy consisting of:
   a. Certainty of profits due to the hedging features involved.
   b. Inflexible space between strikes.
   c. Long and short positions, including both calls and puts.
   d. All calls or all puts, but not a combination of both.
2. The condor is like the butterfly, with the exception that:
   a. Incremental strikes are farther apart.

b. Four strikes are involved rather than three.

c. Several different expiration dates are spread out to exploit time decay.

d. No collateral is required due to the structure that is set up.

3. The hedge matrix describes:

a. Combinations of long and short options over several expiration dates.

b. The use of similar or identical strikes but multiple expiration dates.

c. Combinations of butterflies, condors, and other strategies opened simultaneously.

d. An impossible situation for profits, due to offsetting ITM and OTM positions.

Discussion

Select a company and its stock and set up an example of the 1-2-3 iron butterfly. Examine profit potential based on offsetting long and short positions and the overall net credit.

CHAPTER 8

The Dividend Collar

The dividend collar is a conservative strategy. It eliminates *all* market risk of owning stock and sets up a three-part hedge:

Hedging stock risk is accomplished by purchasing one put per 100 shares. Any decline below the put's strike is offset by increased intrinsic value in the put.

Hedging the put translates to opening a short call, whose premium is used to pay for the put, setting up a no cost of low-cost two-part option position (long put and short call).

Hedging the short call occurs by the purchase of 100 shares of the underlying stock. The short risk is covered, so that exercise of the short call means giving up those 100 shares.

Of course, this three-way hedge requires a working relationship between call and put. If there remains any net debit after opening both positions, it becomes necessary to offset the loss with greater appreciation in the stock. For example, you buy stock at $42 and open two 45 options. You received 0.75 for the call but the put costs 3.00. This is a debit of 2.25 ($225). However, exercise of other option produces a net profit of $300 (strike of 45 less cost of 42). Overall, this is a net profit of $75 ($300 - $225). This means you can afford a debit between the two options if exercise of either creates a net capital gain higher than the debit.

Even so, the "ideal" dividend collar consists of a short call and a long put whose net is zero or a small credit. This is difficult to locate with a strike at or above current value of the underlying stock. As the price of stock declines, the cost of the put rises while the value of the call declines. Examples of a working dividend collar can be found, in which the options net out to zero or better, and exercise produces a small capital gain. The purpose in opening such a position is to ensure earning the current month's dividend without risk of price decline in the stock.

Is this possible? Yes. While dividend collars are difficult to find, they do occur often enough so that you can earn a current dividend every month by rotating in and out of stock positions. In most cases, the parity between call and put will not work, or the price of the underlying stock is too far from the desirable strikes to make the strategy work. However, a diligent examination of ex-dividend dates coming up between today and the next expiration date for options does reveal opportunities that work.

The most practical timing of the dividend collar is when stock is already held in the portfolio and has appreciated in value since purchase. In this case, it is possible to identify a working collar that also builds in a net capital gain in stock in the event the short call is exercised.

This is a difficulty strategy to find without involving appreciated stock. However, the dividend collar is effective as a portfolio management strategy. When you are holding appreciated stock, you are concerned about possible loss if the stock price declines. At the same time, you would prefer to continue holding the stock for further appreciation as well as dividend yield. This is where the dividend collar is worth executing.

Managing Portfolio Profits with the Dividend Collar

Entering a dividend collar with the purchase of stock and trading of both options, all at the same time demands research and patience, but when the right trade is found, it produces double-digit annualized returns.

The three issues in the model portfolio provide examples of how the dividend collar serves as a method for removing market risk and earning the current dividend. These are set up with the assumption that shares were purchased at a price below the current price per share. These are summarized in Table 8.1:

Table 8.1 Three examples of the dividend collar

Symbol	Name	Shares	April 25, 2019 Price ($) Value ($)		January 20, 2016 Price ($) Value ($)		Net gain
T	AT&T	1,400	30.34	42,476	28.55	39,970	2,506
SO	Southern Co.	800	52.44	41,952	39.89	31,912	10,040
MO	Altria	800	51.41	41,128	49.84	39,872	1,256

Table 8.2 Options for dividend collar positions

Symbol	Price ($)	Ex-dividend date	Calls Strike Bid		Puts Strike Ask	
T	30.34	Jul	MAY 30	0.75	MAY 31	0.93
SO	52.44	Aug	JUN 52.50	0.94	JUN 50	0.55
MO	51.41	Jun	JUN 52.50	1.29	JUN 50	1.57

Source: Charles Schwab & Co.

The timing was selected to demonstrate how appreciated value of a portfolio makes it easier to enter a dividend collar position. The dividend collar can be set up as of the later date to protect paper profits and ensure that dividends will be earned in the next cycle. Table 8.2 summarizes a range of available calls and puts and their pricing as of April 25, 2019.

Many options beyond these are also available. However, this set of choices work well for the purposes of the dividend collar to create a risk-free position in the stock (with strikes of options above original basis) at little or no cost.

Each of the choices can be studied to determine the range of outcomes in event of (1) having the short call exercised, (2) rolling the short call forward to avoid exercise, or (3) exercising the long put due to a decline in the stock price.

For example, AT&T was bought at $28.55 per share, and currently is priced at $30.34. This is a paper profit of $2,506 for 1,400 shares. The quarterly dividend is 0.51 per share, or $714 for 1,400 shares. The dilemma here is that you want to protect the $2,506 in profits, but you also want to earn the $714 quarterly dividend. The dividend collar solves this problem with three possible outcomes.

The 31 call moves in the money and the call is exercised. In this outcome:

Capital gain, $2.45 per share, 1,400 shares	$3,430	
Profit on net option credit, 0.75 per share	$1,050	
Total profit	$4,480	

The call moves in the money and the call is rolled forward. In this outcome, the roll delays, avoids exercise, and sets up a credit, which is determined by the premium for the new call. However, this also extends the period of exposure for the covered call.

The put moves in the money as stock price falls, and you exercise the put. In this outcome, the net cost of the options is $18 per share ($93 - $75), or $252. You can exercise at the put's strike of 31 and receive $31 per share or $43,400 versus original cost of $42,476. This creates a capital gain of $924. With the net cost of the collar at $252, this creates a net profit of $672 ($924 - $252).

A similar analysis can be performed for Southern Co. or Altria. The purpose of the dividend collar is to protect current paper profits from appreciated stock (with the long put) and pay for that hedge (with the short call). In all the possible outcomes, several portfolio management advantages are gained:

1. Creation of profits from multiple sources (capital gains, option net credits, dividends, and rolling forward).
2. Downside risk is removed by the long put, which will gain one point in intrinsic value for each point the stock declines below the put's strike.
3. Dividends are earned (except when early exercise occurs), meaning the stock is held risk-free and dividend income is earned as well.
4. The option hedging positions of the dividend collar do not cost anything. In fact, they create net credits, adding to overall net income.

The next chapter moves beyond the conservative strategies based on the combined use of stock and options and explores contingent purchase strategies and rescue strategies, designed to recapture losses and return positions to breakeven or better.

Class questions for discussion and/or mini-case studies

1. The dividend collar sets up:
   a. A three-part hedge involving long stock, long put, and short call.
   b. A two-part hedge in which call and put offset one another, but no stock is owned.
   c. Protection of the dividend through a long put without hedging attributes.
   d. A way to earn dividends without owning stock for any period.

2. In the dividend dollar:

    a. Long calls are paid for with short puts.

    b. Long puts are paid for with short calls.

    c. Puts and calls are both short, generating cash profits.

    d. Puts and calls are both long, paid for with capital gains on stock.

3. Exercise may be a desirable outcome of the dividend collar, when the basis in stock:

    a. Is higher than the strike of the short call.

    b. Is lower than the strike of the short call.

    c. Is as close as possible to the call's strike.

    d. Is matched exactly to the long put's strike.

Discussion

Identify a potentially profitable dividend collar on appreciated stock and explain the three possible outcomes: short call is exercised by someone else, you exercise the long put, or the short call is rolled forward.

CHAPTER 9

Alternatives to Stock Purchase

Options open a range of contingent strategies. Covered calls are interesting because they are the ultimate low-risk form of contingent sale. If exercised, the covered call is designed to produce current income consisting of both dividend income and call premium.

Contingent sale—represented by the covered call strategy—is one of the most conservative uses of options. However, you can also use options to leverage capital in several forms of contingent purchase. As an alternative to buying shares of stock, you can either buy calls or sell puts with the intention of acquiring stock before expiration. This strategy is appropriate when the market is volatile or when marketwide prices have fallen significantly. You recognize the buying opportunity, yet you do not want to risk capital on stock that might continue to fall even more.

Since time is invariably an issue, LEAPS is more likely to work in contingent strategies. The ability to leave positions open for as long as 30 months makes LEAPS well suited for this range of strategies, whereas traditional listed options do not survive long enough for contingency to mature in every case. The risks are simply too great that the option's life will end before stock prices move adequately. This is especially true when you employ contingent strategies with long calls. However, for many, 30-month options will be quite expensive, whereas a 16-month contract may provide enough time for the contingency at an affordable price.

Leverage and Options

The contingent purchase strategy assumes that several conditions exist now:

1. **The market is volatile; prices are down.** The most likely market condition for contingent purchase is when prices have moved downward or are highly volatile. You want to be in the market, but you hesitate to take equity positions, fearing ongoing volatility. The dilemma is a combination of (a) volatile conditions and (b) concern that you will lose opportunities if you don't act now.

2. **You have capital available to open option positions.** You must have capital available either to purchase calls or to leave on margin if short puts are exercised. Looking to the future, if you do decide to exercise long-call positions, you need capital to complete your purchase as well. So, on the long side, you need to be able to buy calls—preferably in several stocks—and later, to exercise. On the short side, you are required to deposit funds to buy stock (equal to the purchase price minus put premium you earn or, on margin, a portion of the purchase price, usually one-half). These requirements naturally limit the extent of contingent purchase in which you can afford to engage at any given time.

3. **You want to open contingent purchase positions in several stocks.** The importance of diversification as a conservative model cannot be overemphasized. The basic theory behind contingent purchase is that you do not know whether a stock will rise or fall in the future, so you select stocks that meet your fundamental criteria and open contingent purchase positions in that range of stocks. If you can afford to engage in contingent purchase on four or five stocks at the same time, you increase your chances that they will end up being profitable. The essential starting point is that stocks you pick must be stocks you would want to purchase if you were simply buying shares. In any contingent purchase strategy, you limit your activity to stocks that meet your conservative standards based on your fundamental criteria.

4. **You believe that contingent purchase, given current circumstances, is an appropriate conservative strategy.** This strategy, like all market strategies, must be assessed in context and as part of a larger portfolio strategy. It is inadvisable to place all your capital in options as part of a

contingent purchase strategy; your conservative portfolio should contain a foundation of strong growth stocks. Contingent purchase can be used to fix the price of additional shares of stock you already own or to ensure your right to buy shares in new stocks if price movement goes in the right direction. But given market conditions and your personal rules for picking stocks, the underlying issues must be appropriate. If you select stocks for contingent purchase based only on option pricing, you violate the basic rules for portfolio management. Conservative investing is always based on equity value of the stock, and options are considered only as a secondary possible strategic means for acquiring shares.

Applications of Contingent Purchase Strategies

Contingent purchase is a way to fix the price of stock if you decide to buy shares in the future (in the case of long calls) or if stock is put to you (in the case of short puts). In either case, the basic rules remain:

1. You would be pleased to acquire stock at the indicated strike price.
2. You can afford to buy the stock.
3. You have performed fundamental analysis and found the company suitable.
4. The contingent purchase strategy is appropriate, and you are comfortable with it as an alternative to simply buying shares at the current price.

Just as any options strategy is wrong when based solely on option premium levels, using contingent purchase without intending to buy stock is wrong. Contingent purchase is appropriate only if you intend to buy shares, and your purpose in employing the strategy should be to limit current risk and not to incur more. If you are following four stocks that meet your criteria, but you are not sure that all will increase in value, contingent purchase allows you to leverage capital among all four while limiting your risk exposure. Even if only some of those stocks increase in value, you can profit from the overall contingent purchase strategy. By fixing premium prices, you keep purchase as one possible outcome without undertaking excessive market risk. You may exercise long calls (or have short puts exercised); the options can expire worthless; or the positions can be closed before expiration.

Contingent purchase strategies require monitoring so that you know when to act and when to wait. This does not mean you have to track prices daily, but frequent monitoring can help you to time subsequent decisions to maximize profits or to reduce undesired losses. Depending on the contingent strategy you employ, time may work for or against you. The use of LEAPS is appropriate given the length of time until expiration, which makes the range of contingent purchase strategies realistic and working with options lasting if 30 months gives you a lot of flexibility. In the market, 30 months is a long time, and a lot can occur in that period. If you look back over the past three years and review the changes in market conditions and prices of individual stocks, you will appreciate the potential of long-term contingent purchase investing.

Even a long position's cost can be mitigated with offsetting long-term short positions as a form of cover. Given the right circumstances, you may recapture the entire cost of the long position without incurring additional risk.

It is risk, when all else is considered, that ultimately determines whether you employ contingent purchase strategies. No matter how profitable and safe a strategy seems to be, it must work as a good fit for your conservative profile. This limits the kinds of strategies you will be willing to use. Option strategies come in all shares and sizes, and many are highly speculative.

If you pick options incorrectly or ignore the underlying risks, using option strategies simply won't work for you. But contingent purchase strategies are sensible and conservative, assuming the following:

1. The fundamentals of the underlying stock meet your standards.
2. You consider the strike price as a good price for the stock.
3. The funds are available to open positions and, later, to exercise.

The Long Call Contingent Purchase Strategy

The first contingent strategy involves buying calls instead of stock. This would be a speculative move if the only purpose was to create profits in call premium. However, if your intention is to buy shares, this strategy fixes your future purchase price at the strike price. If you buy calls in several stocks and only some increase in value, you would exercise those calls only on profitable positions. Contingent purchase limits your capital risk. For example, if you spend $500 on call premium and the stock later falls 15 points, you can never lose more than your $500 investment. However, if you had bought 100 shares of stock in the same circumstances, you would suffer a loss of $1,500. So, the primary advantage of the long-call contingent purchase strategy is limitation of risk. Its primary risk is loss of value, notably time value.

If you buy LEAPS calls with a long time until expiration, which is essential for this to qualify as a conservative strategy, you pay for the time value. The question of whether the contingent purchase is worthwhile is determined by (a) call premium, (b) strike price of the underlying stock, (c) time until expiration, and (d) your desire to fix the price for possible future purchase. One of the more difficult situations occurs when you know that the current price of stock is attractive, but either you cannot afford to buy or you are concerned about short-term volatility. Buying LEAPS calls as a contingent purchase strategy overcomes this dilemma.

Diversifying Exposure with Several Stocks in Play

The strategy should involve several stocks. This diversifies your exposure in a long-option position, and the very reason you are considering contingent purchase is that you do not know what future price levels will be for any stock. Using several well-selected stocks make sense as part of a coordinated strategy.

Here is how a contingent purchase program might work using long calls: a review of the three model portfolio stocks is shown in Table 9.1,

Table 9.1 Stocks for contingent purchase using long calls

Symbol	Price ($)	3-month calls 1 2		9-month calls 1 2	
T	30.34				
Strike 31 32		0.54	0.23	1.40	1.01
SO	52.44				
Strikes 52.50 55		1.01	0.21	2.32	1.28
MO	51.41				
Strikes 50 52.50		2.90	1.49	4.60	3.35

Source: Charles Schwab & Co.

Table 9.2 Buying calls for contingent purchase

Symbol and shares	Price ($)	16-month calls	Total cost ($)
T—1,400	30.34		
Strike 31		1.40	1,960
SO—800	52.44		
Strike 52.50		2.32	1,856
MO—800	51.41		
Strike 52.50		3.35	2,680

Source: Charles Schwab & Co.

which summarizes available LEAPS calls expiring in 9 months (268 days), compared with 3-month (57-day) options.

If you bought calls for each stock, the overall price would depend on the proximity between current market value and strike price. If you compare the strike prices selected for each stock to current market price, you can see how these values change. For example, buying calls to match the number of shares in each stock is specified in Table 9.2.

The total cost of these calls is $6,496. Compared with the cost of $125,556 for shares of each stock, it represents a cost for the calls of 5.2 percent of the price of shares. Contingent purchase is an economical method for fixing the price far into the future. In these examples, over a period of nine months, these long calls fix the price of stock purchase even if the stock price rises far above the strikes. However, for the basic contingent purchase strategy to be profitable, you need a net increase in market value equal to or greater than the investment level. You would need the stock's value to rise above that level to justify the long-call contingent purchase strategy. Although this is a disadvantage, you have a lot of time for the outcome to materialize—nine months in this example.

Reducing Contingent Purchase Risks

Contingent purchase risk can be reduced in a variety of ways. Here are three ideas:

1. **Use a higher strike price.** Table 9.1 listed two strike price levels. If you preferred the second strike over the first strike, your invest-

ment basis would be lower because there would be more points to go before those calls would go ITM. As a result, the higher strike calls are also cheaper.

2. **Invest in longer-term calls.** For example, you gain a full year buying the farthest out calls, which may be as long as 30 months. This provides much more time for these LEAPS calls to go ITM, but these calls will also be more expensive due to the extended time.

3. **Reduce the cost of long calls by using short-call offsets.** The most effective way to cut risks and make contingent purchase a profitable strategy is to write short calls against your long-call positions.

The Covered Long Call

The major risk involved with long-call contingent purchase is the same as for all long-call strategies: If expiration occurs before an adequate price increase occurs in the underlying stock, it is extremely difficult to make a profit. So, risk involves the same problem as every other long-option strategy: Time works against you. Even if the stock's market value rises, you still need to overcome the time value problem.

There is a way to achieve this. If some or all the stocks in this example increase in value before expiration, you can employ a secondary strategy designed to recapture the premium cost of the long call. The basic strategy is to sell a call with a higher strike price and earlier expiration than the long positions. Does this work out?

Assume that you bought the closing strike price nine-month calls for the three model portfolio stocks at the strike immediately above current market value of the stock. You hope that during the next nine months, the price will appreciate enough in these three stocks to make the contingent purchase a profitable strategy. At the same time, you want to get back some or all the money you invested in long LEAPS calls. To make this illustration comparable, assume that all three stocks were to increase between 5 and 10 points soon enough to put the secondary strategy into effect.

Using the Forward Roll Effectively

Rolling forward is attractive when the underlying stock's price is rising. The purpose in rolling is to avoid exercise; it is most desirable to execute a forward roll that creates a net credit whenever possible, defers or avoids exercise, and ideally moves exercise further away from ITM status (up for calls or down for puts). When you have bought a long-term call and cover it with a short call, the short call should expire before the long call.

An alternative is to roll both long and short positions. Roll the short call forward and up to escape ITM status; also roll the long position forward. By closing the current position and opening one with a later expiration, you must pay additional premium. However, if premium levels for the long and short positions offset one another within a close range, this adjustment is worthwhile. You replace the short-call strike price with a new short call 5 points higher. This avoids exercise or, in the event of exercise, creates a 5-point increase in future profit.

Another choice is to replace the current long position with a later expiring call and increase to the next higher strike increment. Since this position is already ITM, you can buy the higher call for an intrinsic value of 5 points. So, although you increase your future purchase price at exercise by 5 points, you save 5 points today by replacing the existing long call with a higher strike price. The four choices in this situation, illustrated in Figure 9.1, are as follows:

1. Roll the short call forward to a later expiring position.
2. Roll the short call forward and up to the next strike increment.
3. Roll the short position forward and up and roll the long position forward.
4. Roll both positions forward and up.

The viability of these rolling techniques depends on current option premium values. As a rule, rolling forward produces higher income because you are "buying" more time. Rolling up is likely to offset that time advantage, especially when you move from ITM to OTM status. In picking a rolling strategy, consider the net balance between credit and debit, compared with the advantages gained by avoiding exercise or changing strike price.

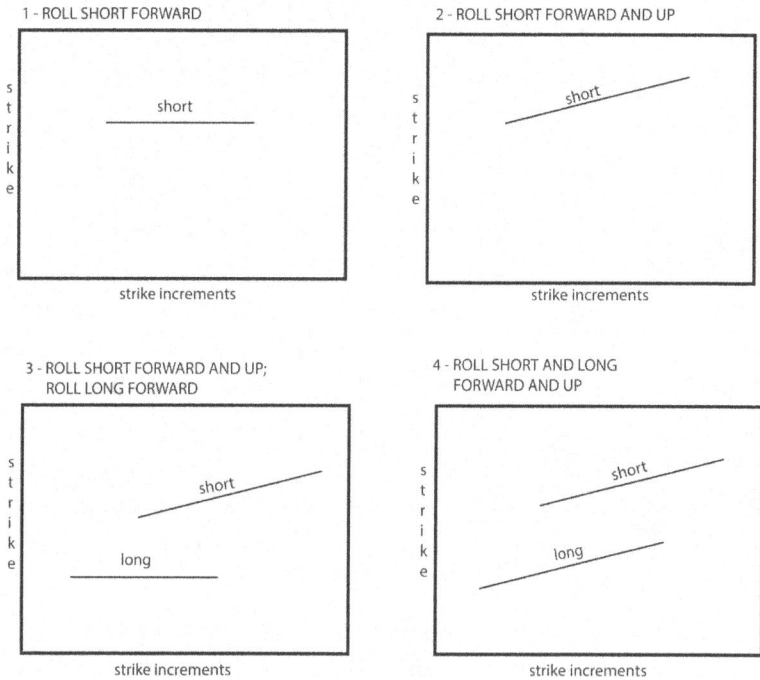

Figure 9.1 *Rolling strategies, contingent purchase cover*

Short Puts and Contingent Purchase

You are not limited to long LEAPS calls to enter a contingent purchase strategy. You can also use short puts. When you sell puts, you are required by your brokerage firm to have adequate funds on deposit to satisfy exercise of the put, if that occurs. The benefit of the put strategy is that money flows to you rather than away from you. Time value is also an advantage. You receive a premium for selling the put, and that premium value declines over time, even when the stock's value falls to ITM price levels. Extrinsic value may offset intrinsic value to a degree for long-term contracts.

Begin with a review of the strike price. If you would be happy to acquire shares at that price, based on the fundamentals, the short put is an excellent strategy. It can go in one of two possible directions. First, the stock does not move ITM, in which case you can later buy the puts to close at a profit or allow them to expire. Second, the stock's market value declines below strike price; in this event, you can either wait for exercise or roll forward and down to avoid or defer exercise. When you roll forward and down, you expose yourself to more time, but you reduce the basis in the event of later exercise by one strike price increment.

The Value of Selling Puts

In the section concerning long calls, diversification was shown to be sensible because the long position was employed. In a strategy with short positions, the same rationale applies in the sense that you do not know which stock will rise and which stock will fall in market value. At the same time, you would not want to acquire shares of all 10 stocks in the model portfolio if current market value declined below the indicated strike price levels. You can use the short-put contingent purchase strategy on any single stock or on a combination of stocks, depending on your willingness to leave funds on deposit and on the attractiveness of this strategy.

If you decided to short puts on all these stocks, you could also vary the strike prices and expiration dates. Table 9.3 presents 29- and 268-day expirations to demonstrate how the time value in short puts can work to your advantage. Although you would not have to select puts with the same expirations, you can judge this strategy by making comparisons.

In determining whether it makes more sense to employ 29- or 268-day puts, you need to observe that the difference in time is nearly eight months. Annualizing returns for each alternative is the only way to fairly compare the two choices and is given in Table 9.4.

Table 9.3 Contingent purchase using short puts

Symbol	Price ($)	29-day bid	268-day bid
T	30.34		
Strike 30		0.35	2.12
SO	52.44		
Strike 50		0.28	1.89
MO	51.41		
Strike 50		1.36	3.90

Source: Charles Schwab & Co.

Table 9.4 Annualized return of short puts

Symbol	Price ($)	29-day calculation	268-day calculation
T	30.34		
Strike 30		(0.35 ÷ 30.34) ÷ 29 * 365 = 14.5%	(2.12 ÷ 30.34) ÷ 268 * 365 = 9.5%
SO	52.44		
Strike 50		(0.28 ÷ 52.44) ÷ 29 * 365 = 6.7%	(1.89 ÷ 52.44) ÷ 268 * 365 = 4.9%
MO	51.41		
Strike 50		(1.36 ÷ 51.41) ÷ 29 * 365 = 33.3%	(3.90 ÷ 51.41) ÷ 268 * 365 = 10.3%

Source: Charles Schwab & Co.

In each case, without exception, the shorter-term puts annualized to a higher net return than the longer-term puts. Although the dollar value of the bids is always greater for longer time to expiration, the shorter-term puts are preferable once returns are annualized.

The Value of Shorter Exposure Terms

Given the shorter time span of the four-month mix of puts, it is preferable to employ these for several reasons:

1. Less time is required for leaving funds on deposit. The money you must leave on deposit in the event of exercise, whether involving one stock or all, will be committed a full year less if you use the shorter expiring options.
2. Turnover profits are higher. By using puts with closer expiration, you are free to repeat this strategy if the short puts expire. As a result, you can create more short-term profits or contingent purchase opportunities.
3. Time value premium declines more rapidly in shorter-term positions. Time value premium tends to evaporate with greater speed in the months prior to expiration than in preceding months. Thus, the 29-day puts lose time value much more rapidly than the 268-day puts. If you determine that it would be better to close and replace

these short positions prior to expiration, it would be more profitable with the 29-day puts.

The same question must be asked for all strategies. Is it conservative? Does this strategy suit your risk profile, and would you be happy to acquire stock based on exercised short puts? Although stock values would be lower than the strike in the event of exercise, your basis would be discounted by the premium received. You would probably want not to enter short contingent purchase positions on a portfolio of 10 stocks at the same time; this example simply illustrates the overall effect of doing so for each stock in the model portfolio. The strategy is more applicable to most situations by looking at a single stock and calculating the likely outcomes based on its price movement.

Rescue Strategies Using Calls

If you sell a put as part of your contingent purchase strategy and the put is exercised, it creates a paper loss. What can you do to recover in this situation?

The solution depends on the point value of the net loss. The first strategy to employ is the roll forward and down to avoid or defer exercise. Even so, if the stock were to continue to decline, it could eventually be exercised. Market prices can fall suddenly, so you do not always have the chance to employ a rolling strategy. Exercise could occur without warning.

Rescue Strategy Based on Smart Stock Choices

When you end up with stock put to you above current market value and your basis still produces a net loss, you have three choices. First, you can simply wait out the market.

Second, you can sell a covered call to offset the paper loss. The danger in the covered call position is that it may be exercised. You do not want to set up a situation in which exercise would create an overall net loss, so premium level of the call must be adequate to offset the paper loss, trading costs, and income tax on your gain. If this is not possible, it makes no sense to write a call.

The third choice is to employ a combination of average-down strategies and short calls. This strategy assumes that you are willing to buy more shares of the stock. Remember, the underlying assumption for all these conservative strategies is that (a) you have prequalified the stock, (b) your hold decision continues to apply, and (c) you would be happy to acquire more shares.

Programming a Profitable Result

There is a tendency to think about stocks in terms of current market value in relation to past market value. If a stock is at $101 per share and over time it falls to $89, the general opinion is that its value has fallen. Value—defined in terms of market price—is a relative idea. However, as the rescue strategy reveals, you can forget about relative value and use options to reduce your basis. This adjusts the perception that the stock has fallen from the original cost of $101 to $89; if you reduce your basis to $84.67 through various options strategies, the realistic gap is only 4.33 points but not 16.33 points. When combined with price averaging, the use of covered calls can turn a loss situation into a smaller paper gap or even into an overall profitable situation.

The Ratio Write: Adjusting to Make It Conservative

A somewhat less conservative strategy is the ratio write. However, risks can be eliminated so that the ratio write fits within the definition of conservative risk. First, an explanation of the unadjusted strategy: The ratio write is a method in which you partially cover your calls. For example, if you own 300 shares and you sell 4 calls, it is a 4-to-3 ratio write. You could view this as having 3 covered calls and 1 uncovered call, or as a 75 percent coverage ratio. The higher the number of shares, the lower the risk. For example, 400 shares with 5 uncovered calls is an approach with less risk than 300 shares with 4 uncovered calls.

The advantage of the ratio write is that it increases premium income with only moderate increase in risk. A variation in the ratio write is to spread strike prices over a range. For example, if your basis in 400 shares of stock is $22 per share, and the stock is now worth $21, you may decide to write 5 calls; you could employ a combination of 2 calls with striking prices of $25 and 3 with later expiring strike prices of $30. The risk is relatively low for two reasons. First, all calls are OTM, and the two upper-level strike prices are 9 points higher than the current market value. Second, two of the calls will expire sooner, and this eliminates all the market risk for the remaining calls, while eliminating the uncovered portion of the ratio write. If the stock's price exceeded the strike price of 25, you could roll forward and up on any or all these positions to avoid exercise.

In this example of the ratio write, the strategy could be rolled forward and up indefinitely to avoid exercise and to keep risks at a manageable level. Even if the 25 calls were exercised, the 30 calls could either be closed or rolled; unless the stock's price soared quickly past the higher strike price, risk of exercise would not be immediate.

Converting the Ratio Write Into a Conservative Strategy

Even with this logic, the ratio write continues to present risks that, on the surface at least, contradict your risk profile. The solution involves using a method for reducing worst-case risk by offsetting the exposed top-side uncovered call. That is achieved by going long on a higher strike price call to offset the uncovered position.

For example, consider a range of options on MO. You bought 800 shares with an original basis of $51.41 per share and the current price one month later (on May 24) was $52.40 per share. You could enter a ratio write with June 52.50 strikes. For example, you could enter a ratio covered call position involving 8 calls, but you could also buy an additional 4 calls for a total of 12. The following represents this strategy:

Sell eight 57-day 52.50 calls @ 1.29	$1,032
Sell four 57-day 55 calls @ 0.51	$204
Net credit	$1,236

In this situation, you have created a combination yielding 3.0 percent return in 57 days ($1,236 ÷ $41,128), which annualizes out at 19.2 percent (3% ÷ 57 * 365). In the worst-case scenario—all short positions exercised—you would be short by 400 shares but with the variety of strikes and you can roll the calls forward or wait out time decay to close some (or all) of the positions early.

The worst-case analysis assumes a rapid increase in the stock's price, necessitating the purchase of "insurance calls" at the top of the transaction (buying long calls to offset risks associated with short calls). However, splitting the ratio between different strike prices provides a degree of protection in most situations. It may not be necessary to assume worst-case outcome and remain within your risk profile range. You may consider this worst case because stock was called away, so the ratio write is appropriate based on the same rules for any form of covered calls: You must be willing to accept exercise as one of the possible outcomes. In the example, using the four long calls at the top of the transaction eliminates the ratio-write risk entirely, while capping any potential loss on exercise of those calls below your original basis.

Ratio Writes for Rescue Strategies and Higher Current Returns

Not only the ratio write is a useful rescue strategy for depressed stock, but it may also serve as a powerful tool for creating higher returns from options with minimal risk, even when the price of the stock is below your original basis. However, to ensure the safety of your position, the split of expiration dates and strike prices is recommended.

Rescue Strategy Using Puts

You can create a rescue strategy with short puts in place of the purchase of additional shares. Short puts can be used as a form of contingent purchase, and an alternate rescue strategy can be employed to reduce average price while creating additional downside protection through put premium income.

The Risk of Continued Price Declines

The difference in this variety of the rescue strategy is that there is a further chance for price decline. Therefore, you should employ such a strategy only when acquisition of more shares is desirable based on your fundamental analysis of the stock. If additional short puts are exercised, you could revert to the original rescue strategy and write covered calls. However, using short puts allows you to create a lower net basis in stock without necessarily having to acquire more shares. If the short puts expire, you create a reduced basis in the original 100 shares by virtue of put premium.

In the worst-case outcome, you increase the number of shares owned. The advantage of having more shares is clear: Profits would be three times those of the 100-share rescue. However, using short puts may be more conservative because you would not be required to buy shares unless prices decline below strike price. Given that average share prices have a continually reduced basis, the question becomes "are you willing to buy more shares as market prices decline?" If you believe that the stock's long-term value remains strong, this may be desirable; or you may conclude that as strong an investment as it is, there is simply too much volatility. You would prefer, then, to create a situation in which the net basis is lower than the current market value so you can sell shares at a profit. The stark outcome used to seem unlikely, but the large declines in stock values in 2008 and 2009, even of companies once considered quite safe, make the point that you must live with risk if you are in the market. The advantage with options strategies over simple ownership of stock is found in the hedging or mitigation of market risk. You have stock-based market risk simply by owning stock. Options reduce or eliminate the risk.

Both varieties of the rescue strategy achieve your goal of reducing exposure and recapturing paper losses. If you can reduce your basis to create a profitable outcome, the rescue strategies are valuable ways to manage your portfolio. The decision to use calls or puts depends on your attitude toward the company, available resources, and your willingness to wait out the stock's market trends.

Covered Calls for Contingent Sale

Looking beyond contingent purchase, you may also want to consider contingent sale strategies. The most conservative form of contingent sale is the covered call. When you own 100 shares and you sell a call, you invite the possibility of exercise. One strategy—writing deep ITM calls to create exercise intentionally—makes sense, but only if you first consider the tax implications.

Writing deep ITM calls has a potential tax consequence. You could lose long-term capital gains treatment by writing what are called unqualified covered calls, those more than one strike increment below the current value of the stock. Before entering a strategy like this, you need to analyze the tax consequences.

Picking the Right Conditions for Forced Exercise

The strategy of creating a forced exercise as a form of contingent sale makes sense under two conditions. First, your original basis in the stock should be low enough that the exercise price would create a profit. Second is awareness of the tax rules. When you sell ITM covered calls, you may lose long-term status for taxing of capital gains. In the event of exercise, the entire transaction could be taxed at the short-term rate. The difference in long-term and short-term rates could be substantial, perhaps even offsetting the option premium with increased tax liability. However, if you have a significant capital loss carryover, current-year short-term gains will be absorbed by the carryover loss. In fact, creating current-year gains may be a smart tax move, because annual loss limitations are only $3,000, and it could take many years to completely use up a capital loss carryover. For some unfortunate ex-stockholders of Enron, WorldCom, or any number of dot-com stocks that lost half of their value in 2008, the carryover loss may never be entirely absorbed unless future gains are realized to offset those losses from year to year.

One of the great advantages to covered call writing is the ability to use well-selected stock as cover for a string of covered call profits. This strategy—based on the fundamental value of the stocks in your portfolio—enables you to keep stock in most circumstances, while enhancing current income. This can work over many years if you write OTM calls, use high-dividend stocks, reinvest your short-term income, and avoid exercise. If stock is worth holding onto for the long term, it is worth avoiding exercise through a series of rolls forward and up. The forward roll increases the time value, while rollup increases the strike price so that if exercise does occur later, you will increase your stock profit by that point spread as well.

The possible alternatives to outright stock purchase demonstrate how you can use options to leverage your capital, employ conservative techniques to offset time value risks, and put rescue strategies into effect when a stock's price moves downward. The covered long-LEAPS-call strategy even employs shorter expiring short calls to balance out long-position time value. All these strategies make it possible to deal with volatile market conditions, improve your portfolio diversification, and lock in prices on a range of stocks that you might want to buy soon.

The next chapter expands on these concepts to show how options can offset paper losses and maximize conditions in down markets.

Class questions for discussion and/or mini-case studies

1. A contingent sale based on covered calls is developed with:
   a. 100 shares and 1 short call, set up to accept exercise at a profit.
   b. An uncovered call to generate current income adequate to afford to buy shares.
   c. A short sale of shares offset by ownership of a long call to hedge the risk.
   d. All of the above.

2. LEAPS options used in contingent strategies:
   a. Are not advantageous due to high time value.
   b. Provide benefits with long calls, but not with long puts.
   c. Add flexibility with a longer term until expiration.
   d. Present certain tax problems that must be overcome.

3. Long call and long put contingent strategies are costly, but the cost can be reduced by:
   a. Buying cheaper contracts OTM without exception.
   b. Focusing on lower-priced stocks to reduce the cost of options.
   c. Selling shorter expiration options to pay for the long options.
   d. Using capital gains to pay for the options, even if that means being uncovered.

Discussion

Identify methods for reducing the contingent purchase risks based on LEAPS options. Discuss the benefits or problems of each method.

CHAPTER 10

Option Strategies in Down Markets

Some options strategies qualify as conservative, if the purpose is to manage and hedge the portfolio rather than to simply speculate. You can use long puts or calls to manage price change, and short puts—with their limited risk—present great opportunities if they are used solely when you would be happy to acquire more shares of the underlying stock.

The chronic problem every investor faces is the inevitability of cycles. The stock market experiences these cycles in numerous ways. The severity and duration of a cycle determines the success of your program, if only because timing is so crucial. Even though you invest with the long term in mind, you prefer to adhere to the advice to buy low and sell high, instead of the other way around. Chapter 9 showed how to devise a rescue strategy when stocks move in an unexpected direction as part of a contingent-purchase plan. In this chapter, you find a variety of additional option strategies worth considering.

Thinking Outside the Market Box

What characterizes the "crowd mentality" of the market? Fear and greed often have more to do with decision making than does prudent or analytical, strategic thinking. Although an academic approach—often taken by someone with no money at risk—dictates against fear and greed, it is more difficult to ignore those emotional responses to market trends when you have capital at risk.

Knowing this, how can you proceed? Fundamental data is less exciting than current-day price movement and far more difficult to convey in a 10-second television or radio news bite. Most news that investors receive through television and radio is useless. The print media are more useful to the extent that stories go into greater depth and may be more analytical. Coverage by the leading financial newspapers and magazines is superior to television and radio media, primarily because the venue is more suited to the kind of fundamental and analytical information you need.

Remembering the Fundamentals

The success of a conservative approach to investing is based partially on the quality of research and information available. You may use one or more of the dozens of free Internet websites and subscription services; print services, including newspapers and magazines; and stock market services. The amount of time and money you spend determines how information-based your decisions are; ultimately, going directly to a company's website and reviewing quarterly and annual financial statements is a fine starting point. This assumes that you can glean information from the financial reports provided.

A sensible way to narrow your field of investigation is to identify a few high-quality fundamental indicators and then investigate companies meeting your criteria. This is preferable to listening to analysts and Wall Street personalities and then buying stocks they recommend, often without fundamental reasons for doing so.

If you want to act as a contrarian in the way you pick stocks, you must first ask yourself "is the market efficient?" If so, does the majority tend to make sensible market decisions? In fact, the majority often does not make good decisions, so a contrarian approach to stock selection makes sense. It may be the ultimate contrarian approach to define yourself as a conservative investor and at the same time use options to manage market price swings.

The long-term conservative point of view is that taking a long stock position in well-chosen companies is the primary, and perhaps the only, method for investing success. Most refer to this approach as value investing. However, this approach may not be conservative at all. If you entrust your portfolio to short-term price gyrations, you are at the mercy of a chaotic and ever-changing market. It makes more sense to view your portfolio in two segments. First, the foundation of your conservative portfolio will always be defined with well-selected companies whose long-term value ultimately dictates where their stock prices will head. Attributes of such companies include consistent growth in dividend payments, strong and consistent capitalization, and competitive growth in revenues accompanied by consistent earnings. Second, you can manage market gyrations with the selective use of options, which is prudent and conservative if the purpose in using options is not speculative and if option richness does not dictate which stocks you hold or buy. Options help manage market volatility, increase short-term profits through hedging strategies, and devise rescue strategies when your portfolio experiences paper losses. All these goals are conservative.

Conservative Versus Speculative: Remembering the Difference

Timing is crucial in the use of options. A speculator is likely to devise strategies and select options based primarily on implied volatility and a perception of how stocks will react in the short term. However, because speculators leverage their capital in high-risk scenarios, they do not appreciate long-term goals as a priority. The uses of options in the two instances—speculative and conservative—are vastly different. You use options successfully if you time strategies to take advantage of short-term price changes in stocks you own, to protect paper profits, or to average prices when your stock values have declined but you continue to believe those companies as quality investments.

Options can help you to overcome the short-term timing problem, enabling you to acquire more shares when prices are low. When prices are high, options are effective at protecting paper profits without having to sell shares.

The Long Put: The Overlooked Option

The tendency to favor long calls over long puts—a common phenomenon among speculators—arises from the tendency for investors to be optimistic. Realistically, you know that market values rise and fall, but those who speculate in long options invariably believe that a stock's price will begin rising immediately after they buy a call. It is not common for speculators to consider buying puts in the belief that the stock will fall in value.

This generalization applies to most, but not all, speculators. However, since so much emphasis is placed on calls, long puts are often overlooked and at times undervalued as a result. Your conservative risk profile may present situations in which buying long puts not only makes sense but also conforms to your standards.

When the Stock's Price Rises

Two scenarios are worth considering. First, and most likely, is one in which a stock's price rises quickly. The temptation is to sell shares at the market top and take profits. This is a dilemma. You want to keep shares for the long term, but you also want to protect paper profits. If you don't want to sell shares, buying long puts is a sensible alternative. You do not need to spend a lot of money on long puts either. If you expect a correction within two to three months, you can probably find an OTM put for a relatively small premium with a two- to three-month expiration. Buying longer-expiring puts provides longer terms of insurance and profit protection.

For example, assume that you purchased shares of various stocks and they have appreciated. Use the model portfolio to summarize available ask prices of long puts expiring in 57 days (about 3 months) and 268 days (about 9 months), as shown in Table 10.1.

Low-cost puts can be used to protect profits. If you have bought shares of stocks that tend to rise and fall on average with prevailing overall

Table 10.1 Long puts to protect paper profits

Company	Symbol	Price ($)	57-day puts 1 2		268-day puts 1 2	
AT&T	T	30.34				
	Strikes 29 30		0.32	1.10	1.82	2.87
Southern	SO	52.44				
	Strikes 52.50 55		1.49	3.35	3.20	4.70
Altria	MO	51.41				
	Strikes 52.50 55		2.96	4.85	5.75	7.35

Source: Charles Schwab & Co.

market direction, a rapid price increase could create an overbought position in many, if not all, of your portfolio issues. So, the use of puts to protect paper profits is a prudent strategy for managing your portfolio with short-term price trends in mind. Rapid price spikes tend to correct within a short timeframe, so if you have read the market correctly, this strategy—even given its limited life span—is both realistic and conservative. Shorter-term options provide protection for shorter time periods, often with advantageous pricing.

Depending on the amount of time you want to have the protection, premium cost varies considerably. Balancing time and cost enables you to identify a practical means for managing short-term price fluctuation in your long stock positions. The alternative is to ignore short-term price gyrations and simply hold stocks for long-term appreciation. This is also a conservative approach. Since short-term price movement is often irrational and not caused by any fundamental changes in the companies themselves, you can either avoid management of short-term price changes or use options to exploit price spikes and to create the opportunity for additional profits without substantial capital risk.

The strategy of buying puts to insure paper profits (or even to provide a safe floor for your purchase price of shares) is a system for managing short-term volatility while continuing to execute the long-term conservative policies you have established in your portfolio. This is not mere speculation; it is a method for protecting current value at a relatively small cost, just as is purchasing fire and casualty insurance on your home even though the chances of a loss are slim. In the case of your portfolio, it is doubtful that properly selected stocks will experience large price declines, but when market prices rise too quickly a short-term correction presents an opportunity to protect profits for a relatively small cost.

When the Stock's Price Falls

In the second scenario, long puts are used when market prices fall rapidly. In this situation, you may recognize a buying opportunity, but you also fear further declines. You use long puts to provide an immediate floor for stocks in your portfolio. In cases of extreme short-term volatility, you can combine long puts with long calls. Long puts protect your capital value in case of a further decline; at the same time, a price rebound would make the long calls profitable.

The two scenarios for using long puts—when your stock prices either rise or fall rapidly—are based on the premise that you want to protect the value of shares you own and want to keep. This qualifies both strategic uses of long puts as conservative in nature. Speculators have no interest in protecting long stock value; in fact, the true speculator does not even own stock unless it serves as a vehicle for executing some related strategies such as covered call writing. Were you to play market price swings, you would be defined as a speculator. However, the strategies described here are designed to serve as insurance for your paper profits, reduction of further losses, or an opportunity to take paper profits if they materialize. The thoughtful selection of long puts makes sense in these extreme market environments. It can also make sense to buy puts for insurance. For example, if you buy shares and want to guarantee that the market value will not fall below your net basis, using puts as insurance is wise even when market prices are not especially volatile. It is conservative to insure long positions. A basic assumption is that your stocks will rise in value. Realistically, you also know that you could be wrong, at least in the short or intermediate term.

Short Puts: A Variety of Strategies

When you sell puts, you receive the premium payment. If the stock's market value falls below strike price, the put is exercised. You can avoid exercise by rolling forward and down, or you can accept exercise and have 100 shares put to you. However, in down markets, selling puts can be a valuable method for acquiring additional shares of stocks at a reduced price, thus reducing your basis in stock through the profits you earn from shorting puts.

Is this a conservative strategy? Opening uncovered options is almost universally considered high risk, but in fact the market risk for short puts is identical to the market risk of covered calls. Some important differences apply, of course. Table 10.2 summarizes and compares covered calls to uncovered puts.

These points demonstrate that the market risks are identical, but important differences are present as well. A covered call that expires can

Table 10.2 Covered calls and uncovered puts

Description	Covered calls	Uncovered puts
Margin or cash deposit required	50% of stock price	Collateral equal to 20% of strike value minus premium received
Stock price rises	Above strike, call will be exercised; to avoid exercise, the call can be rolled forward	Put will lose value and eventually will expire worthless; after expiration, another put can be sold
Stock price falls	Stock loses market value and short call will expire worthless. If price falls below net value (stock price minus option premium), a paper loss results. A replacement covered call below net basis would cause a loss if exercised	Put gains market value and may be exercised, creating a net loss identical to a loss on stock; however, the put can be rolled forward and replaced indefinitely and at any strike
Dividends	Dividends are owned as long as stock is owned	There is no stock ownership, and dividends are not earned

be replaced, but the net basis must be kept in mind to avoid opening a call that, if exercised, will create a net loss. However, with the short put, the position can be closed to avoid exercise and replaced with a later-expiring put of any strike. An ITM put can be replaced with a lower OTM put and since no stock positions are involved, it does not matter. This flexibility gives a significant advantage to the uncovered put strategy.

Conservative Ground Rules for Short Puts

Following are seven conservative ground rules for selling puts in down markets:

1. **Sell puts on stocks you already own.** Conservative standards state that you will buy and hold stock that meets your fundamental criteria.
2. **Select strike prices based on support level.** The stocks you select for writing puts, like all stocks, are likely to trade in a predictable price range.
3. **Sell puts that provide a minimal rate of return.** What rate of return will you earn on short puts if exercised?

4. **Coordinate the strike price and current market value.** In picking short puts, you want to gain the best possible premium, but you also want to avoid exercise.

5. **Pick the expiration time based on your market perceptions.** How long should you leave yourself exposed in the short position? The longer the expiration, the greater the time value; the shorter that time, the lower the risk.

6. **Pick exit levels or roll levels when you initiate the transaction.** You may set a bailout or profit-taking rule for yourself.

7. **Plan secondary strategies in the event of exercise.** What if the price of the stock falls below the strike price, and before you can roll out of the position, the put is exercised? In that case, you need a rescue strategy.

Three Rescue Strategies

A conservative strategy develops a contingency plan to rescue the stock if your put is exercised. (This is comparable with an exit strategy or other contingency plan you employ in managing your portfolio even if you don't use options.) If the short put is exercised, it means current market value will be below the strike price, you would end up with more shares at a reduced basis from your original cost but at a basis above current market value. Your rescue strategy in this case may take three forms:

1. **Take no further action.** You can wait out the market in the belief that although the downward price movement is lasting longer than you thought, the stock's value will rebound.

2. **Sell short puts again.** You can repeat the strategy in the belief that the price level is lower than the stock's long-term support.

3. **Sell covered calls.** You have acquired additional shares, and this provides the potential to revert to a covered call strategy.

Using Calls in Down Markets

Using puts to average down your basis and acquire more shares—or to increase income when those short puts are not exercised—is one way to manage your portfolio in a down market. You can also use calls based on the same arguments.

Long calls can maximize your position if you remember these guidelines:

1. **Buy calls on stocks already qualified or owned.** The conservative use of long calls must be based on the fundamental value of the underlying stock.
2. **Buy calls only when the stock's price is low.** Timing is everything with options.
3. **Identify and define an exit strategy.** When will you close the long-call position?
4. **Select strike prices with your intent in mind.** You should select a strike price you consider an attractive price for the stock based on the trading range prior to the price decline.
5. **Coordinate cost and expiration so that the strategy is logical.** In picking long calls in down markets, limit the premium cost, because all the premium is in time value.

Calls Used for Leverage, but Not for Speculation

The selection of calls in your conservative portfolio is a matter of leverage rather than speculation. The difference is based on ownership of the stock or on restricting the activity to the short list of stocks you have analyzed and qualified. It makes sense to have a list of stocks you would purchase if given the chance, and a price decline is the perfect opportunity to buy shares—assuming you are right about the timing and extent of the decline itself. Given this uncertainty, using long calls is more conservative than putting a large sum of capital into the purchase of shares. With calls, your potential loss is limited to call premium, and the potential profit is theoretically unlimited. When you buy stock, the same profit potential exists, but you risk further price decline if you time market volatility incorrectly.

You can employ ratio-writing techniques in down markets to speed up your recovery and to close the gap between net basis and current market value. For example, if you own 800 shares and you write 10 calls, your ratio will produce more income than strict one-to-one coverage provides.

(You eliminate the uncovered call risk by purchasing a higher long call.) Although ratio writing is one method to rescue paper loss positions, with well-chosen stocks your premise for holding them is a belief that prices will recover soon. Other rescue techniques are more prudent and contain less market risk; a ratio write may turn out to be a poor strategy if the stock's market value rises more rapidly than you expected, and you end up exiting the position through exercise of stock you would rather keep.

Rescue Strategies and Opportunities

A conservative options strategy makes sense as part of a rescue strategy or to take advantage of down market buying opportunities. Such opportunities are often best dealt with using options because it is more conservative than buying more stock. Timing, in all investment strategies, is both the key to profits and the potential gateway to losses. However, conservative investors, referring faithfully to in-depth analysis of the fundamentals, are less likely to fall victim to short-term price changes. Your decisions, if based on conservative investing standards and well-understood fundamental indicators, will likely be more successful than the average technical investor's, because you do not buy into short-term trends; you prefer to exploit those trends to find real bargains in market pricing.

Another question must be asked, however: Have the fundamentals changed? Among the many causes of stock-specific volatility, a plateau of a growth trend is one of the many signals that a growth period is slowing down or even stopping. All trends eventually flatten out; nothing continues in the same direction forever.

Stock Positions and Risk Evaluation

If you want to coordinate your portfolio management requirements by using options, you must first classify risks and keep them in perspective. Inexperienced options traders commonly forget to pay attention to stock fundamentals, picking options in isolation. Even if a speculator uses only long-option positions and never buys or sells stock, fundamental analysis invariably affects (a) the success of an option trade; (b) pricing trends based on support, resistance, and overbought or oversold conditions; and (c) timing of purchase and sell decisions for options.

Risk evaluation of stock based on both price volatility and fundamental volatility (levels of period-to-period changes in revenue and earnings trends) is at the heart of risk analysis. The two types of analysis—technical and fundamental—are directly related and have a cause and effect on one another. The tendency to look at only one set of indicators is a mistake because to truly understand the causes of market trends, you need both.

The Relationship Between Stock Safety and Options

The stronger the fundamentals for a company, the safer your selection of options. A stock whose price volatility makes it high risk is also invariably a high fundamental risk. Companies are unlikely to have safe fundamentals but high-risk technical indicators, or vice versa. The two go hand in hand. The same point applies to option strategies. If your stocks are selected based on corporate strength, excellence of management, strong revenue and earnings trends, dividend history, and competitive stance within a sector, the option choices will match the stock's fundamental strength.

Some down market conditions indicate that your best course of action is simply to sell. Cut your losses and invest capital in other companies whose value is greater and whose long-term growth prospects are more promising. Accepting losses is part of investing in the market, and few people will suggest that any line of strategies can make your portfolio foolproof. You will continue to have losses in the future, just as you have in the past. However, well-selected option strategies can protect you against losses, help you solidify paper profits, improve short-term income, and reduce your basis in stock positions—all without having to assume higher levels of market risk.

Examining Your Risk Profile

Even when you have defined yourself as conservative, it can be instructive to review your attitude toward long positions in stocks. There are three likely points of view, and you may even hold these views in different ways for different issues in your portfolio:

1. **Long-term hold for conservative stock growth.** The traditional conservative view is that you should select stocks based on long-term value, growth potential, dividend record, and capital strength; keep them for the long term; and use them to build wealth over many years. This ideal continues to provide an intelligent investing method for many individuals.

2. **A vehicle for current income via covered calls.** Many investors select stocks using sound conservative principles, but with the primary idea of earning consistent current income from writing covered calls. This is also a sound investment program. It is entirely possible to earn option-generated current income with no added market risk, as demonstrated in Chapter 6. This strategy works best when stocks have been picked using sound fundamental analysis associated with conservative investing.

3. **A combination, the best of both worlds: long-term value investing with potentially high current returns.** If your portfolio consists of carefully picked stocks of value that offer long-term growth potential, you can also generate current returns with covered call writing.

Options and Downside Risk

Using calls in down markets limits the degree of losses caused by further downside movement. Premium earned for writing covered calls reduces net basis in stock, which also helps close the gap between basis and current market value. Long puts or long calls provide profitable outcomes if stock prices move enough in the desired direction; the problem with long-option positions is twofold. First, time works against you when you buy options. Second, time value declines as expiration approaches, requiring far more price movement in the stock to justify the decision to go long in the option.

The Down Market Benefits of Options

There are four primary down market benefits of options, which you can use to manage your portfolio:

1. **Short positions reduce your basis in stock.** The first benefit worth analysis is that short options produce income, which reduces your basis in stock.

2. **Short-put premium reduces overall basis in the event of exercise.** Writing short puts produces income and, possibly, allows you to accept exercise if the stock continues to decline.

3. **Repetitive covered call writing increases current income while cushioning risk range.** Writing covered calls on existing stock positions also helps to protect against paper loss, even in a down market.

4. **Downside risk is also reduced with price averaging.** When a short put is exercised, you end up with reduced-basis stock.

Option Planning with Loss Carryover

One troubling aspect of using options in down markets is the possible tax effect. If you create capital gains through exercise, those gains are taxable. Do you prefer reversing paper profits or deferring taxable gains? A lot of emphasis is placed on tax deferral, but you are better off accepting additional tax this year if that tax results from creating net profits.

The alternative—holding on to shares of stock whose basis is higher than current market value—affects your current investment return and, in some cases, traps you in a losing portfolio position. If you can use options to change the course of profits, you are far better off. For example, assume that your effective tax rate (federal and state combined) is 40 percent. All additional income you generate will be taxed at the 40 percent rate, and your after-tax profit will be the remaining 60 percent. In this condition, are you better off waiting?

If your income is high enough this year that you would prefer to take profits in the future, you can avoid creating additional profits from options. However, the outcome of that decision is zero additional profits.

If you can create additional earnings on your investment portfolio, you are ahead with a net 60 percent, compared with no profit at all.

Current-year profits can also be sheltered entirely if you have a large carryover loss. With a limitation of $3,000 maximum net loss deduction per year, you may need many years to absorb your loss. One solution is to generate profits in conservative strategies this year. Another is to offset current-year gains against losses in stocks you want to dispose of without option activity. A third is to invite exercise by writing deep ITM covered calls to dispose of stock at a sure profit and to absorb a part of the carryover. In this situation, the loss of long-term status is not a concern because your purpose is to dispose of stock and to use up the carryover loss.

Timing: Matching Current-Year Profits and Losses

If you face a large capital gains event this year, be careful to avoid writing ITM covered calls, which may put your long-term gain status in jeopardy. Such a consequence can be suffered unintentionally. For example, if you roll a short call forward and create an ITM situation without realizing its consequences, and then the call is exercised, you could end up with a large short-term gain instead of a long-term gain. The resulting tax liability could more than offset any option profits you earned in the strategy.

A carryover loss should be viewed as both an investment portfolio problem and an opportunity. It is a problem because it represents a zero return on your investment. You can use only $3,000 per year, so if you are working with a $30,000 net loss, it will take 10 years to realize the full benefit, and a $90,000 loss would take 30 years to absorb if you had no gains in ensuing years. This situation is an advantage because you are free to realize year-to-year gains without worrying about the tax consequences. Timing of sales does not matter, because your profits will be absorbed to the extent of the loss carryover. The sooner you absorb the carryover loss, the greater the benefits. In taxation, the concept of deferring liabilities while accelerating benefits is well understood. It is like calculations of internal rate of return. You maximize your earnings by compounding your return, avoiding idle cash or other value (and "value" can include the benefit of sheltered gains) and seeking maximum gain without additional risk. So, a large carryover loss presents flexibility in the timing of current-year profits.

Taxes complicate the calculation of net gain. This makes it necessary to think about all the aspects of gain and loss on a net of taxes basis. A marginal gain can turn out to be a net loss if you do not plan. With taxes and trading costs in mind, some options traders prefer to trade in blocks of options rather than in single contracts. The question of how many contracts to use is a complex one for your conservative approach to options. It depends largely on the number of shares you own and the additional number you would like to acquire. The strategies employing single contracts can be easily applied in multiples. Risks are identical if the relationship between the number of shares and the number of options remains the same, at least on the short position. When you consider using long options, the question of risk changes. The more contracts you buy, the greater your exposure to market risk, so you need to balance the dollar amount of risk with the potential benefits in long options and understand the tax rules in any option strategy you use.

The next chapter explains conservative combination strategies involving options. These can dramatically reduce your basis in stock while creating current returns with options and without incurring added market risk.

Class questions for discussion and/or mini-case studies

1. The difference between speculation and conservative strategies is:
   a. Speculators tend to gain higher net profits.
   b. Speculators are more imaginative than conservative investors.
   c. Conservative investors seek protection of capital, and speculators take more risks.
   d. Speculators use options and conservative investors never do.
2. Long puts are best used when:
   a. The underlying price rises quickly and is expected to retreat.
   b. Prices are on the decline and are expected to rise soon.
   c. Long calls have proven unprofitable.
   d. Underlying shares are not held and won't be in the future.
3. Rescue strategies may consist of:
   a. Taking no action and waiting out the price cycle.
   b. Selling short puts.

    c. Selling covered calls.

    d. All the above.

Discussion

Highlight the similarities and differences between covered calls and uncovered puts and discuss both in terms of risk and potential net income.

CHAPTER 11

Combination Conservative Techniques

Options traders employ a variety of strategies, combining options in short and long positions, hoping for various forms of price movement (or lack of movement), and hedging other positions in stock, both long and short. Most of these strategies are inappropriate for your portfolio. However, some combinations can provide a valuable way to maximize your income from options without added market risk.

Many of these strategies have always been available on short-term options but considered impractical because expiration invariably occurred too soon. With the advent of LEAPS, the entire options picture has changed. Since LEAPS options last up to 30 months, advanced strategies have moved from the realm of theory into the realm of practicality. For speculators, this means that it is possible to take greater risks and create combinations with potential for higher-than-average earnings or losses. For conservative investors, the availability of long-term options increases the current income potential with less concern for pending expiration.

In this chapter, the various types of combinations are analyzed to provide a complete background and explanation of the range of possibilities and to create examples of some interesting conservative strategies that do meet your conservative profile: the creation of higher-than-average returns without a corresponding increase in market risk.

Spread Techniques

The first popular strategy is the spread: the opening of two or more option positions on the same stock, involving different expiration dates or different strike prices. A more complex spread involves both different expiration and strike features.

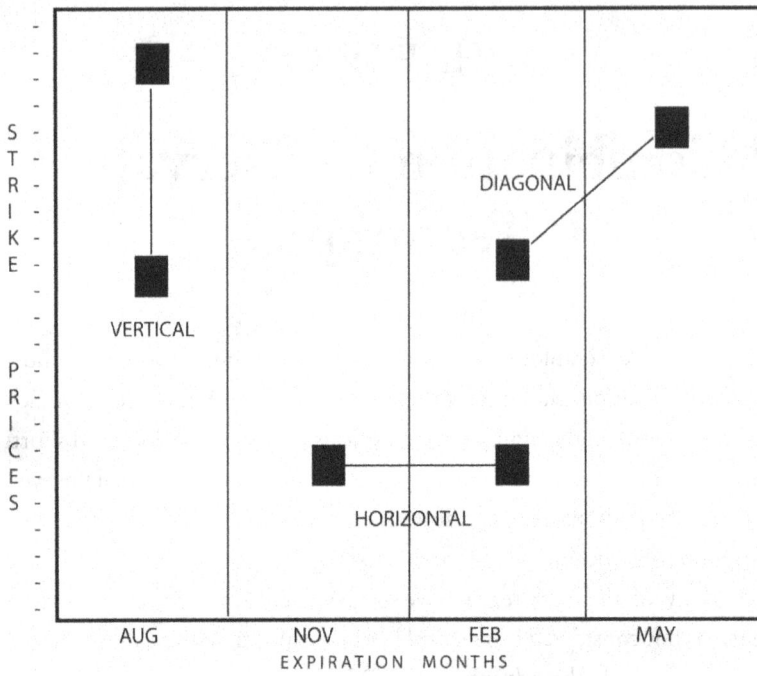

Figure 11.1 Types of spreads

The options industry has its own range of specialized terms, each used to communicate specific strategies and positions. For example, a spread can be described as vertical, horizontal, or diagonal. A vertical spread has different strike prices but the same expiration date. A horizontal spread is the opposite: It contains the same strike price but different expiration dates. A diagonal spread has different strike prices and different expirations. These three spreads are compared side by side in Figure 11.1.

By viewing the shape in each type of spread, you get an idea of how these strategies work. The spread is distinguished in other ways as well. For example, a bull spread is one designed to work out profitably if the value of the underlying stock rises. In comparison, a bear spread is maximized when the underlying stock's value declines. A box spread is the simultaneous opening of a bull spread and a bear spread. The use of any of these spreads depends on the direction of price movement you expect to see in the stock between the opening date and the expiration date. However, because you must spend money (for long positions) or expose yourself to market risk (for short positions), a spread—with a few exceptions—is usually not appropriate for your conservative portfolio. The selection of long options whose premium is greater than the premium from any short options in the spread is called a debit spread (in other words, you must pay money to open the position). The reverse situation—the use of short positions exclusively, or of short positions whose total premium receipts are higher than the cost of long positions—is called a credit spread.

Advanced Spread Terminology

The terminology is even more complex than these basic definitions. For example, a ratio calendar spread is any spread in which the long and short positions are not identical in number. As part of a complex rescue strategy, for example, you may open a series of long calls in the belief that the stock will rise, and you may offset a portion of those long calls by writing higher strike price short calls. This reduces the overall cost but still enables you to benefit from upward price movement. A ratio calendar combination spread involves a ratio of a greater number of long and short options with a box spread. A conservative use of options rarely employs this advanced strategy. However, it is possible to end up with complex strategies by opening a series of simpler options at various times. The point is that while you are wise to know about the full range of option strategies, you will probably never use them.

One final advanced spread is called the butterfly spread. This strategy has three parts: open options within a strike price range, offset by other options at both higher and lower strike price ranges. The purpose of the butterfly is to limit losses in exchange for limited profits. It is difficult to justify such positions, and they often result from a series of less complex decisions over a period and in reaction to price movement in the underlying stock. The transaction cost of opening positions with limited profit also makes complex spreads unproductive.

Straddle Techniques

Whereas the spread involves variation of strike price, expiration date, or both, the straddle requires that strike price and expiration are the same. To open a straddle, you buy an equal number of calls and puts (a long straddle) or sell an equal number of calls and puts (a short straddle); in either case, the option positions would have the same strike price and expiration date.

With a long straddle, you experience a loss in the middle range, represented by a point spread on either side of the strike price, and profits either above or below that range. For example, if the total cost of opening a long spread is 11 ($1,100), then the stock must move either up or down by 11 points for you to break even. Anything beyond that range is profitable, and if the stock's price remains within the 11-point range until expiration the position becomes an overall loss. You can close one side of the position without closing the other. For example, if the price of the underlying stock moved up enough points to make the calls profitable, it could be closed, and the puts left open. The same argument is true on the downside. Puts could be closed, and calls left open. In writing a long straddle, the best possible outcome would be price movement in both directions, enough so that each side can be profitable in turn. The long straddle is highly speculative.

Short Straddles for Conservative Positions and High Rates of Return

The short straddle involves opening two short positions with the same strike price and expiration. An equal number of calls and puts produces a middle-range profit zone with potential loss zones above and below. For example, if you receive a net premium of 9 by opening a short straddle, your profit zone is 9 points on either side of the strike price; above or below that range, you face a loss. The troubling aspect of the short straddle is that you are always ATM or ITM on one side or the other, so exercise is always a possibility. You can roll forward and up with the short call to avoid exercise, and you can roll forward and down with the short put. If you own shares of the underlying stock and you write no more than one call per 100 shares, the risks in this position are minimal because the short call is covered. If you do not own 100 shares, the short straddle is high risk, a combination of both a short call and a short put.

The short straddle with ownership of the underlying stock is one variation of the contingency strategies covered in Chapter 9. It involves a contingent sale of stock you own (the covered call) with a contingent purchase of additional shares (the uncovered put). Since premium income can be substantial in this combined strategy, the short straddle can serve as a viable conservative strategy.

Mixing the Long and the Short

An example using combinations of options is the opening of a long call and a short put in a down market. This provides multiple benefits. First, the cost of the long call should be offset by the income from writing the short put. Second, if the stock declines further in value and the short put is exercised, your basis in the stock is averaged down. The average basis consists of the average price between original purchase of shares and the strike price of newly acquired shares minus put premium. Third, if the stock does rise, you can either close the call at a profit or exercise it and buy additional shares below market price, further reducing your average basis in the stock. This strategy—assuming you would be satisfied if the short put was exercised—is conservative. It involves low cost or zero cost (in some cases, even a small credit), and it is advantageous under any scenario of price movement. Even no movement would be satisfactory, considering that the combined strategy is a zero-cost one.

Using long puts to insure paper profits against the possibility of price decline is a sensible strategy by itself. But consider yet another variation combining long and short options: the long put and short call combination. In this instance, you achieve downside protection in two ways. First, the long put would match ITM intrinsic price movement dollar for dollar. This put can be exercised and shares sold above market value, or it can be closed to take paper profits without selling shares, a highly desirable attribute of the insurance strategy. Second, the covered call offsets all or part of the long put cost, so that you end up with free downside protection, and it may reduce your basis in the stock to the extent that the short premium of the call exceeds the long premium of the put. Time works to the advantage of the short position; the covered call can be closed at a profit, allowed to expire worthless or allowed to exercise. You can also roll forward and up to avoid exercise if the stock's price continues to rise.

These are only some examples of how you can continue to manage your portfolio on a conservative basis using options in combination, enabling you to take appropriate action in three market conditions:

1. In up markets, protecting or realizing paper profits without having to sell stock
2. In low-volatility markets, increasing current income with covered calls
3. In down markets, averaging down your basis and turning paper losses into paper profits or realized profit

Theory versus Practice

Using options in your long-term portfolio works if you structure that use within the guidelines of your conservative risk profile and consider all possible outcomes. For example, whenever you go short on calls or puts, you should fully understand the consequences of exercise.

The requirement for a conservative application of options is that any and all strategies should involve stock that you have qualified under your risk standards, that you either own or want to own, and that you consider an attractive long-term investment. Nonconservative option strategies tend to be overly complex and although they may work out on paper, they do not always produce the high rates of return that seem so easy. Stocks do not always move in the desired direction, or quickly enough, for high-risk strategies to become profitable. Speculators—especially inexperienced ones—often pay too much attention to the profit potential of complex option combinations and far too little to the associated high risks. In especially complex option strategies, the minimal loss is often offset by a related minimal profit.

Simplicity as a Worthy Goal

One conservative principle worth adopting is this: Keep it simple. The fallback position for any options strategy is to return to the basic conservative theme: Select high-quality growth stocks and hold for the long term, selling only if the fundamentals change. If any options strategy is overly complex or difficult to understand, avoid it without exception. You can use conservative strategies to protect paper profits, offset depressed markets, and employ for contingent purchase; you do not need to extend your risk range because an options strategy would require it.

Risk analysis is an essential part of the informed options strategy. This is the process by which you determine whether a strategy is appropriate, given the range of risks involved. The analysis also includes evaluating the outcomes that may occur and then comparing potential return to the potential market risk and other risks (e.g., lost opportunity risk).

In performing a risk analysis, the worst-case outcome must be considered in deciding whether to proceed. Actual outcome comparisons are difficult because one involves selling stock and another does not; the purpose of analyzing outcomes must be to ensure that in any possible event, you are satisfied with that outcome. For example, if you are thinking about writing puts in a down market, the worst-case outcome is a continued decline in the stock. Writing puts qualifies as a conservative strategy if you have already determined the following:

1. The stock is a good value at current levels.
2. The strike price would be attractive if the put was exercised.
3. Premium income is high enough to justify the short position.
4. You will get an attractive averaging down of basis if the put is exercised.
5. You would like to acquire additional shares of the stock.

Tax Problems with Combination Strategies

The complexity of combination strategies is only one of the problems you must sort through. As a conservative investor, you may prefer simplicity, if only because basic conservative strategies involve fewer risks. The possible tax consequences may also discourage you from involvement with complex strategies.

Some forms of combinations create an unintentional wash sale, so profits or losses you intend to recognize in one tax year could be disallowed. Any "offsetting position" that creates a straddle could result in the loss of long-term capital gains status for long stock. The Internal Revenue Service (IRS) definition of offsetting positions in which it could occur requires a "substantial diminution of risk of loss" for the capital gains penalty to apply. By definition, a conservative straddle makes sense only if it reduces your risk exposure, and under the tax rules you do not have to cover stock to fall within the definition of having an offsetting position.

The Anti-Straddle Rule and Its Effect

The tax rules set up the potential consequence that the transaction will be negated under the 30-day wash-sale rule. You could also lose long-term capital gains status on stock sold, and the deferral of deduction for losses. If, by definition, a current-year loss is offset by a successor position (e.g., a related second side of a straddle), the losses could be deferred and deducted from the basis in that successor position. This limitation applies to the loss on an option position, the expense of executing transactions, and applicable margin interest.

The so-called "anti-straddle rules" in the tax code are complex and designed to discourage the use of options to create current-year losses to offset future-year gains. However, the complexity of these rules may discourage you from considering complex straddles as a viable part in your conservative portfolio. The complexity itself is a form of risk—tax complexity risk—that makes advanced options troubling.

You can also create an "unqualified covered call" unintentionally when you roll forward to avoid exercise. If you become involved with advanced options, including ITM covered calls or straddle positions, you should first consult with a tax professional who understands the current tax rules and question whether any use of options that may complicate the tax status of long-term stock is worth the tax complexity risk. Even if you use expert help in preparing your tax return and in planning investment income each year, the special rules concerning these option transactions change everything. You may not simply be able to pick a strategy and proceed, without knowing how it will affect your tax status.

The Ultimate High-Return Strategy

It is wise to shun any overly complex strategies that are unclear as to risk levels or that contain unintended tax consequences. There is a difference between investors who appreciate simplicity and those who are attracted to the exotic, the complex, and the difficult to understand. Some option trading takes place for the enjoyment of the complexity rather than for a desire for profits.

One strategy is especially appealing because it creates an immediate return, it is not complicated, and market risks are not increased. A straddle involves the simultaneous opening of a call and a put with identical strike prices and expiration dates. By modifying the straddle, you can create a short position without facing the near certainty of exercise. Instead of employing identical strike prices, this involves the use of OTM strikes to create a short combination made up of covered calls and uncovered puts.

A Review of Your Conservative Assumptions

For the modified straddle to work, observe the following 10 rules:

1. **You are willing to accept exercise of the covered call.** As with all conservative strategies involving short options, you must be prepared for exercise.
2. **Exercise of the call will result in a profit in the stock.** There is never a reason to open a covered call position if exercise would create a loss.
3. **You are willing to accept exercise of the uncovered put.** You also need to acknowledge that the short put could be exercised.
4. **You have funds available to buy shares if the put is exercised.** Your broker requires that you have funds available to complete this transaction if the put is exercised.
5. **You consider the put's strike price a good price for stock.** The put's strike price should, in your opinion, be desirable.
6. **The strike prices are selected with the stock's trading range in mind.** Your review of this strategy should be coordinated with a study of the stock's recent trading range history.
7. **Premium income from both positions is attractive.** To justify any option position, the premium levels must be right.
8. **The proximity of strike prices to current market value is ideal.** The current market value of stock should ideally reside exactly half-

way between the strike prices of the call and the put, or within one point of the halfway mark.

9. **Fundamental analysis of the underlying stock has passed your review.** It is essential to evaluate the stock before deciding to buy shares or to continue holding shares you already own.

10. **You have evaluated all possible outcomes, and you are satisfied that this strategy is worth entering.** Consider all possible outcomes, including the net portfolio value when the stock declines below the put's strike price and you end up with a paper loss.

Compare Yields

If calls are exercised, you gain points between current market value and strike price. The exercised rate of annualized return is calculated based on current market value; also consider your original basis in each stock as part of the process to determine whether, in your opinion, this combined strategy is worth the exposure.

The return will also be different if either option or both options decline in value and are closed or if you replace them by rolling forward and up (calls) or forward and down (puts). These variables point out the difficulty in making accurate comparisons between stocks and between outcomes.

This analysis is only accurate on the assumption that all options expire worthless. The return will be quite different if one or both options are exercised. The point spread for the combined short position can also become important.

Either short option can be rolled to avoid exercise if the stock's price rises above the call strike or below the put's strike; you can roll forward and up (for the call) or down (for the put) to expand your non-exercise zone.

Outcome Scenarios

Even if you identify a desirable yield from options strategies, it still makes sense to go through the possibilities to make sure that you understand what could occur and what actions if any, you would want to take in response.

Planning for Each Outcome Scenario

Consider what actions to be taken in the following scenarios:

1. **The trading range of the stock remains between the strike prices.** If the stock's trading range remains below the call strike price and above the put strike price, neither will be exercised.
2. **Both options are exercised.** If price in the underlying stock moves enough points ITM on both sides, you could experience exercise of both options.
3. **The call is exercised but the put is not.** In this situation, your stock is called away at the strike, but you are not required to repurchase those shares.
4. **The put is exercised but the call is not.** If the put is exercised, you acquire an additional 100 shares.
5. **The stock's market value falls below the put strike and remains there.** This is the worst outcome of all—whether you write short options or not.

The Augmented Strategy: A Short Straddle

Using the previous analysis, what happens if you write a straddle instead of creating a spread with its strike price gap? You do this when you would find it most desirable to have either or both options exercised. If you write a straddle as close as possible to the current market value of the stock, you could create a potentially high premium value in the options.

How the Dollar Values Alone Can Mislead

Annualized return and dividend yield are the key indicators for valid and accurate comparisons. In the short straddle, you create consistently high current returns on an annualized basis; however, it is also likely that one short position or the other will be exercised. If you accept the premise that exercise of either the call or the put (or both) would be desirable, this straddle is impressive. The strategy works best when the short call and put strikes are as close as possible to the current market value of the underlying stock.

If stock price moves above or below breakeven, the loss consists of exercised options and loss of 100 shares (from exercised call) or acquisition of an additional 100 shares (from exercised put). Both outcomes can be avoided by rolling short calls forward to later strikes (or to higher call strikes or lower put strikes).

Maximum Advantage: Large-Point Discounts

It remains possible to roll out of these short positions, depending on the direction of price movement. In the event of rolling forward, the OTM short option loses time value and can be closed at a profit or allowed to expire. There is also the chance that ITM short positions could be closed at a profit due to erosion of non-intrinsic premium.

Rolling to avoid exercise extends exposure time and also increases profit potential. The short straddle is conservative as long as the usual qualifications apply: You want to keep shares of stock and add to your holdings; you have qualified the stock in fundamental terms; and you consider the put strike price (discounted by short option premium) a fair price level for the stock.

The next chapter presents a review of risk, and specifically explains how to evaluate risk in an options-based portfolio.

Class questions for discussion and/or mini-case studies

1. Spreads come in many varieties. These include:
   a. ownership of stock spread with a short option.
   b. vertical, horizontal, or diagonal.
   c. covered by combining short and long, but only when opened vertically.
   d. stock-based or option-based spreads.
2. Straddles contain specific characteristics, including:
   a. opening a call and a put at the same strike and expiration.
   b. ensuring that both sides are OTM.
   c. preferring ITM options to increase net income.
   d. high income even for long positions.

3. A short straddle can be conservative when:

a. the distance between strikes is quite small.

b. the underlying stock is highly volatile.

c. different strikes are used.

d. 100 shares are owned to cover the short call side of the trade.

Discussion

Research and explain three tax issues involving options trading: the wash-sale rule, anti-straddle rule, and unqualified covered calls.

CHAPTER 12

Risk Evaluation Techniques

Conservative investors must define levels of risk as the means for selecting appropriate strategies. However, "risk" is not a singular factor. There are many types of risk to be concerned with, and not all of these relate specifically to options. Many forms of risk apply to the dilemma of picking investments that yield acceptable rates of return, but with a low enough risk to qualify. This "zone of risk/profit" is narrow. This chapter examines the many forms of risk and demonstrates why options are not the problem but may provide the solution to the risk question.

Options belong in the conservative portfolio, not solely as a money-making set of strategies but also as a portfolio and risk management tool, generally meaning as a hedging device. The options strategies explained and demonstrated in this book can all be profitable, but they serve the dual role of creating profits while reducing risks.

This does not mean that options address every form of risk, and it certainly does not ensure that options traders follow their own goals and "rules" for when to exit positions. The temptation to hold off closing and taking profits or cutting losses is compelling, and this may well be the most serious form of risk that may be called "greed" risk.

The Nature of Greed Risk

The problem every trader faces is how to manage profits. "Greed risk" comes into play when profits materialize rapidly. Even though you know you should get out and take profits immediately, you are also tempted to wait because you might earn even more profits. But in those cases when the profits evaporate (which happens often if only due to time decay), the opportunity is easily lost.

The same issue arises when a position loses value. You might start out setting the policy that you will close and take losses if an option loses 50 percent of its value. But when it happens, the same "voice of greed" presents a stubborn alternative: Don't take any action but wait for the trend to reverse and take you back to a zero loss position. This is ill-advised.

Following sensible rules for taking profits and cutting losses is easy advice to give, but more difficult to follow. Every options trader is subject to greed risk, but a programmed response for taking profits or cutting losses ultimately leads to a higher overall profitability in the portfolio. In a conservative application, options trading are not only about profit or loss, but also about risk mitigation. Having this in mind—protecting long equity positions with sensible options trades to reduce basis, offset market risk, or provide secondary rescue strategies—is essential in a conservative portfolio.

A Range of Option-Related Risks

Like most products, options trading involves a series of risk. The best-known risk (market risk) is also the most obvious, but some traders focus on this alone and may be less aware of the many other forms of risk every investor and trader faces. However, market risk is a good place to start because it exists in all trading and investing.

Market Risk

Market risk in its most basic form is that the value of a position will decline. For most investors, this occurs when a position is opened and then loses value. For short position options traders, it also occurs when the underlying value moves in the wrong direction (up in price for short calls, and down in price for short puts). Opening any product position involves market risk specific to that company or its products and derivatives.

Market risk is also called "systematic risk" and refers to marketwide declines, affecting all positions held by an investor or trader. Here again, the most common version of it is for an investor with a long position to lose due to overall bearish movement. The same applies to traders holding short positions when markets move against those positions.

Both versions are the same type of risk, but the causes of unfavorable movement may be specific to a product or company or applied to the entire market.

Information Risk

Another way that traders deal with risk is in the quality or reliability of information they receive and act upon. If you make trades based on what you read or hear in the financial press, you cannot know with certainty whether that information is reliable. Since it is often expressed in sound bites of only a few seconds, financial news tends to be simplified to what the journalist believes to be the main points.

Information risk applies even if you develop your own sources for timing of trades. If you rely on chart analysis, you are going to make trades based on subjective analysis of price trends, reversal signals, and confirmation. Naturally, you bring a bias to the process and this is unavoidable. No one should expect to be able to act objectively in interpreting price movement, and even if you could, the chance for error still exists. It is a risk, and the only way to avoid it is to take no action.

Collateral Risk

The requirement that you provide collateral in a margin account can present an unpleasant surprise in many circumstances. When you enter a trade, you must ensure that you have adequate capital in your margin account. For long options, you are simply required to pay for the option. For short options not covered by long positions, collateral is equal to 20 percent of the exercise value minus premium received.

Options trading "margin" is a completely different aspect to trading than the better-known margin account for equity positions. If you buy stock on margin, you can borrow up to 50 percent of the cost, leveraging the purchase and increasing potential profits as well as risk. But for options, "margin" is not a device for leveraging, but a requirement to cover risks.

Disruption in Trading Risks

Trading can be halted at any time and due to any number of reasons. A big single-day decline in markets can bring on a trading halt for the remainder of that day; in some cases, individual companies are halted due to a high level of volume based on takeover rumors and other news.

For options traders, a halt in trading can adversely affect the outcome of a trade. The desire to close a position is not normally affected by current market news, but a trading halt also applies to options trades, so all trading is suspended until the halt is lifted.

Brokerage Risks

For most options traders, an online discount broker makes sense because commissions are cheap. However, beyond that, an options trader is expected to possess a level of experience and knowledge to make trades without the help of a broker.

An options trader relying on advice from a broker faces a specific risk. If that broker is not experienced enough to provide sound advice, then all trades are exposed to risks. No one is going to take care with someone else's money that they would take with their own. If you rely on a broker's advice for options trades, the question you may want to ask is whether you really need outside advice. Not only does it make no sense to rely on someone else, but it exposes you to brokerage risks.

Trading Cost Risks

If you calculate a profit zone for a series of trades, the calculation must include an estimate of trading costs. A marginal profit can be wiped out or even turned into a loss by the costs of entering and exiting a trade.

For many, this risk is overcome by trading multiple contracts. A single option trade will average about $5 to open and another $5 to close. But the structure of commissions is to add a small additional fee for each option, such as 75 cents. One option costs $5 but 10 will cost about $12. It comes out to only $1.20 per option.

Trading costs affect profits, but placing more capital at risk only to reduce the average price per option may introduce a higher risk exposure as well. This is a balancing act between the cost of trading and the exposure with the number of options traded. This also brings up collateral risks if short positions are part of a trade.

Unavailability of Market Risk

Options traders generally assume that they can buy and sell whenever they want, but this is not always the case. In some cases, markets are unavailable. If you trade directly with a broker using your phone lines, a day with unusually heavy volume means that you won't be able to place your trade when you want. Today, most options traders use automated online trading systems and those trades go through in a matter of seconds; some traders still prefer the more expensive but personal contact with the trading desk. This is where the unavailability risk is involved.

Another version of "unavailability" may be called "illiquidity risk." Even though bid and ask prices of options are listed in brokerage websites, check the open interest and volume of trading for each option. If there are no open contracts and no trades, you probably will not be able to get the prices listed; those represent the latest information but not the actual market price you should expect to transact.

Lost Opportunity Risks

When you commit capital to a position, one aspect not found in the numbers is the lost opportunity. For example, covered calls are attractive and properly structured; they yield double digit annualized return; and all likely outcomes are more profitable than just holding stock. However, covered calls and similar hedged positions also involved lost opportunity.

For example, once a covered call is opened the stock price might move far above the strike, and shares will be called away. If you had owned shares without writing a covered call, you would have made a larger profit.

The way to think about lost opportunity risk is to evaluate whether it is acceptable or not. Considering that a large price rise is going to happen occasionally, but covered call profits are a constant, it is often acceptable to live with the occasional loss of shares at a fixed strike below market value. But you can only be happy with covered call writing if you are able to live with lost opportunity risk and not to look back with regret when shares are called away.

Lost opportunity risk also refers to missing out on an attractive trade because your capital is fully committed elsewhere. It does not mean that part of your investment portfolio should be kept in the form of cash, but it does mean that no one can take advantage of all trades. There will always be a degree of lost opportunity.

Inflation and Tax Risk

One of the most dramatic forms of risk relates to all investing and trading and demonstrates why conservative options strategies make sense. The combination of inflation and taxes define what you really need to earn just to break even, and it is probably much higher than many traders think.

To determine your breakeven yield—the yield you need to simply preserve the value of your investment dollars considering inflation and taxes—use the following formula:

$I \div (100 - R) = B$

where I = inflation rate, R = effective tax rate, and B = breakeven rate.

The inflation rate is the rate currently in effect as measured by the Consumer Price Index (CPI), or the rate you expect to experience next year.

The effective tax rate is the rate of tax you must pay on your overall income, and the rate that would apply to any additional earnings. It should include both federal and state taxes combined. For example, if your last year tax rate was 33 percent federal and 8 percent state, your overall effective tax rate is 41 percent. If you assume inflation in the coming year will be 3 percent, the breakeven formula is:

$3 \div (100 - 41) = 5.1\%$

It reveals that you must earn at least 5.1 percent on your investments just to match inflation and taxes. If you make a lower yield than this, you are losing money after inflation and taxes. Some conservative investors assume that lower yields are always safer, so they settle for extremely low returns to avoid risk. But if their yield is lower than the breakeven level, they are losing money, which is not at all conservative.

The solution is to use conservative options strategies designed to produce yields above the breakeven rate. This means risks are kept under control, but you earn enough to beat inflation and taxes.

Estimating Your Risk Tolerance

Your risk tolerance is affected by many factors, which might also change over time and with evolving life circumstances (marriage, having children, changing careers, income levels rising). Factors affecting risk tolerance include:

1. **Knowledge and experience.** Options trading must be based on knowledge or experience, or you are not qualified to embark on the many ways to hedge risk and manage your portfolio. You can gain knowledge and experience by starting out with some very basic strategies using limited capital or by virtual trading to learn the mechanics of trading.

2. **Income and assets.** The level of your income and available assets must also influence your risk tolerance. Younger singles and newlyweds often have very limited resources, and it is not until they build a base of assets and begin earning higher income that trading in options will make sense.

3. **Family issues.** A single person has different risk tolerance than a married couple. When children are born, risk tolerance changes once again. Family issues are constantly evolving just based on these factors. On the negative side, ill health, divorce, or death affect risk tolerance, perhaps even more.

4. **Individual goals.** Not everyone invests or saves for the same reasons. You might be saving for a child's college education, a safe retirement, or starting your own business, just to list a few of the goals that will influence risk tolerance levels.

5. **Your age.** As much as anything else, age is a big factor. A young, single trader with the so-called "disposable" income is likely to act more recklessly than an older, more experienced trader who has had losses in the past but cannot afford big losses in the future. Age affects risk tolerance in terms of years of trading experience, maturity, and knowledge.

The next chapter examines a final step in the development of a conservative portfolio: stock selection. Many discussions of options trading focus only on the option, but a conservative trader will want to build a foundation of options trades based on both conservative strategies and the use of high-quality stocks.

Class Questions for Discussion and/or Mini-Case Studies

1. The term "greed risk" refers to a tendency among investors to:
    a. want profits all the time even when making bad decisions.
    b. increase holdings as prices rise, expecting the rise to continue.
    c. over-diversify to profit from many positions.
    d. take steps to reduce or avoid taxes on profits.
2. Information risk is:
    a. made worse than ever with a broad availability of information, not all of which is true.
    b. not a big factor in the modern day due to efficiency in the market and the Internet.
    c. a reference to forgetting to rely on published books and articles for new ideas.
    d. seen in complex markets like options or futures, but not in the stock market.
3. Lost opportunity risk:
    a. refers to missed investments because capital is already committed.
    b. occurs with covered calls when the underlying price rises and profits are lost.
    c. may be the consequence of failing to act when profitable ideas are presented.
    d. all of the above.

Discussion

Explain how breakeven is properly calculated in the investment portfolio, and which factors are present; also explain why it is essential to find investments that represent suitable and acceptable levels of risk, while meeting or exceeding breakeven return.

CHAPTER 13

Stock Selection and the Option Contract

When all possible options strategies are considered in the context of your conservative profile, what are the criteria for determining which (if any) strategies are appropriate? A recurring theme in this book is focusing on risk profiles and remaining faithful to your original conservative investing themes, limitations, and capabilities.

No options strategy is appropriate if its use requires you to alter your risk profile. However, if you discover while investigating options that you are willing and able to take on higher risks than you had assumed previously, you need to reevaluate all your underlying assumptions. The process of defining risk tolerance is an evolving process; few investors keep the same risk profile without change over time. Risk level is determined by a broad range of other matters: knowledge and experience, personal income and capital, change of job, marriage, birth of a child, divorce, death of a family member, and changes in a family member's health.

Your Conservative Profile as a Priority

Even with a thorough grounding in options and their context, you need to continually remind yourself of your personal goals, limitations, and standards. The market is a playground full of temptations, and many well-intended investors become distracted from their sensible goals and drawn to the dangerous but exciting high-risk, exotic, and potentially profitable schemes that are so visible and popular. Conservative, fundamentally based strategies are not terribly exciting, especially in the media-focused market environment. The media tend to emphasize index movement, substantial point change in high-profile stocks, and market rumors and news. Even fundamental news like earnings reports is focused on variation between analysts' predictions and actual outcome rather than on the value of the company as a long-term investment. This scorekeeping is the popular game on Wall Street— at the expense of less exciting but more relevant strategies based on fundamental analysis.

The market, as a media-driven "store" containing an array of products (stocks, bonds, commodities, and derivatives), is distracting. It is very much an open market with brokers tempting buyers with promises of easy riches. Little if any attention is paid to the analytical, detail-oriented fundamental study of a company's financial statements and other financial information. Why should the media highlight a subtle change in a capitalization or working capital ratio? It is much easier to report a 2-cent variation between earnings and predictions or a 4-point movement in the stock's price.

Pitfalls in Using Options

Options, like so many aspects of the market, offer numerous temptations. The speculator is drawn to the positive aspects: leverage of capital with the potential for fast profits, often in triple digits, and the fast pace of the market. They rarely pay attention to the other attributes of risk associated with options: equally fast losses, long-position disadvantages, and the virtual impossibility of profiting from speculation consistently.

It is easy to lose sight of your goals. You can slip out of a conservative mode, allowing risks to expand unintentionally, and become fascinated with the potential of an options strategy. The importance of testing every strategic choice against the sound, conservative risk profile you have already established in your portfolio serves as a standard for selection.

Allocation by Risk Profile

Some people believe that a sensible way to use options is to create a base in their portfolio at some percentage of capital. For example, they may devote 80 percent of their capital to conservative investments. The remaining 20 percent is "mad money," put aside to give in to temptation and to seek high returns along with high risk. However, it is a poor policy. Why not invest 100 percent of your portfolio in high-value stocks and then use options conservatively to augment returns, protect long stock positions, and take advantage of market price overreactions? It makes more sense. You will experience consistent current yields using strategies like contingent purchase, covered calls, and short combinations (involving covered calls and uncovered puts). These uses of options do not add to market risk. Their overall theme is easily summarized: They are designed to provide conservative returns consistently over time. Of course, you will occasionally have shares of stock called away with short calls or have shares put to you with short puts, and you may lose the opportunity to make a higher profit if you had made different choices—the value of hindsight. In exchange for the occasional lost opportunity, you can modify your portfolio to create option returns, a trade-off you may view as a good choice most of the time.

These strategies must always conform to your long-term conservative risk profile. Your purpose is to build wealth, not to speculate recklessly; so the use of options must be restricted to those strategies that enhance your existing long stock positions or that expose you to the purchase of stock that you desire to own —either more shares of existing issues or shares of other stocks that have been prequalified as appropriate for your portfolio.

Some people, notably those who have not examined the conservative potential in the options market, argue against the concept that options augment the conservative attributes of your portfolio. One conclusion is impossible to avoid: Not only are some option strategies conservative, but also not employing them puts your portfolio at greater risk. For example, when a stock's market value rises far above its normal trading range, you naturally expect a short-term correction. This is the perfect time to write covered calls. You expect the stock's value to retreat, but if strike price is properly selected with current higher-than-expected prices in mind, exercise itself would create a substantial profit. If, instead, you buy puts for insurance, you also protect paper profits by timing your decision based on awareness of trading range versus current price spikes. The same observation is true when prices decline rapidly. A downward spike is a buying opportunity. The traditional method, buying additional shares, is a difficult decision to make when prices have fallen because you may be uncertain about short-term volatility and potential for further decline. An alternative is to buy calls or, even more conservatively, to sell OTM puts.

In either event, you create the potential to buy more shares and average down your basis in the stock without placing more capital at risk through purchase of shares.

Using Options to Reduce Market Risk

The ultimate conservative approach, the short combination or short straddle explained in Chapter 8, creates a position in which even a drastic decline can be rescued with additional options positions. When you create a large protective range through the selection of options strategies, you reduce market risk rather than increase it. In many instances, just holding shares and taking no action becomes high risk, even in a conservative portfolio. The long-term approach traditionally has shunned strategies based on reaction to short-term price movement in favor of holding onto conservative growth investments. This plan works; however, average returns on a conservative portfolio are less than 10 percent. Options can help you to adhere to your conservative risk profile while also beating the market consistently.

You have heard wild promises about double-digit and even triple-digit returns by applying an investing "system" of one kind or another. Experience (meaning "loss") has taught you that schemes do not work and that there are no easy or sure-fire ways to beat the market. Even the conservative use of options requires diligence, learning techniques, mastering terminology, and becoming more knowledgeable than the average investor. Some conservative investors are content to buy shares in blue chips and to place the balance of their capital in a moderate growth mutual fund. Although this traditional approach may enable you to experience average growth or even to outperform long-term averages, it is not spectacular.

Temptation to Select Most Volatile Stocks

When your conservative portfolio does not perform as you expect, what can you do? Some investors are tempted to sell lackluster stocks and go with more exciting, more volatile issues. The idea is that you can experience profits more rapidly, make up for past losses, and outperform the market. In fact, though, this approach is an abandonment of conservative principles. You need to continue to carefully select value stocks and then protect their equity value. This is the conservative strategy.

Investors who like the idea of using options also face danger when they pick stocks inappropriate for the conservative risk profile. If you shop option premiums with the idea of buying stock and then discounting your purchase price with covered calls, you are taking the wrong approach. A conservative application of options requires that you first select stocks based on fundamental analysis and comparison; that you pick stocks with lower-than-average volatility and potential for price appreciation; and that the capital structure, revenue and earnings, PE ratio, dividend history, and other indicators of your stocks are a good fit for your conservative standards. Then you use conservative options strategies to protect equity and enhance current income. Using conservative options strategies on risky, volatile stocks contradicts your standards. The first rule is to pick your stocks carefully and then identify methods for protecting their value.

Creating a List of Potential Investments

There is no shortage of high-quality stocks. By applying conservative principles, you can easily identify at least 10–20 stocks you would like to own. You might not be able to afford to buy shares of all of them, but it is not the point. Once you develop your list of quality growth investments, you can buy shares in several of those companies; if a covered call strategy ends up with stock called away, it is not a complete loss. The transaction frees up capital that can be reinvested in the stock of another company on your list.

You gain further flexibility in options trading when you own more than 100 shares of stock. It gives you the chance to vary the use of options, to cover partial holdings, and to change the mix of short options against long stock when you roll forward and up. You can also write covered calls with a mix of expiration and strike prices or make combinations and short straddles more flexible and interesting with a similar mix.

Creating Sensible Conservative Standards

If you accept certain options strategies as fitting within your conservative framework, it is worth asking again: What is the definition of a conservative portfolio? In other words, what are the basic standards for stock selection? You already know that picking stocks based on potential option premium levels is a mistake that should not enter the equation.

The Four Conservative Standards for Stock Selection

There are a few well-understood conservative standards for picking stocks. These should include, at the very least, the following four criteria:

1. **Revenue and earnings trends.** The quarterly and annual rate of growth in revenues and consistency in earnings is always a sound starting point in fundamental analysis.
2. **Capitalization and working capital.** If a company is depending increasingly on long-term debt to fund growth, an increasing portion of future earnings will have to go to debt service, leaving less capital for expanded operations and dividend payments.
3. **PE ratio trends.** The PE ratio combines technical (price) and fundamental (earnings) in a single multiplier.
4. **Dividend history.** The history of dividend payments and the current yield are indicators pointing to growth and working capital management.

This list is only a starting point—the bare minimum of fundamental indicators. In your conservative analysis, you may also use any number of other indicators you find useful, including a broad range of balance sheet or income statement ratios, management indicators, or combinations of fundamental and technical trends.

Maintaining Fundamental Clarity

Investors tend to believe that good values are difficult to find. However, confusion arises to define "value" in the market. Some investors think that they should buy stocks that double in value immediately after they purchase shares. This is simply unrealistic. But even conservative investors may end up chasing short-term profits and may conclude that it is difficult to find profits—by a double-in-value definition—with consistency.

Under a conservative standard, quality investment is defined as a strongly capitalized, well-managed, profitable, and competitive company whose stock has performed strongly and consistently, and whose fundamental and technical risks are a good match for your conservative profile. Under this definition, there are many good values to be found in the market. The argument against covered call writing—that you risk losing stock if exercised—is often premised on the idea that a stock, once lost, cannot be replaced. In fact, though, good values abound and can be located using fundamental criteria.

Distinctions: Risk Standards versus Brand Loyalty

The clarity with which you view your long-term goals has everything to do with how you manage your portfolio. Investors often develop a "brand loyalty" to the stocks they own. Closely related to this is an aversion to some companies based on non-investing criteria. For example, some people hate Wal-Mart or Microsoft and will never buy shares in those companies. Some investors are faithful to IBM or Pepsi. These love-or-hate opinions are not often based on fundamental analysis but on some personal, social, or political opinion. To maintain clarity, avoid investing in companies that you either love or hate, if only because strong feelings about a company can cloud judgment. You can make more objective decisions about when to buy, hold, or sell a company's stock if you are neutral about its policies, politics, or social impact. For example, if you once owned a small retail store and you were forced out of business because Wal-Mart opened a Supercenter across the street, you may not be able to objectively evaluate the investment value of Wal-Mart stock. If you swear by Microsoft products, you might not be able to analyze the company's ability to compete in the market.

Given the large number of excellent quality investments, it makes sense to limit your analysis to those companies that you can evaluate objectively. In stock selection as well as in a decision to employ options strategies, there is plenty of fundamental analysis to be done without struggling with personal feelings about the company itself. If you have personal conflicts about a company, avoid buying shares and restrict your search to those companies that you do not find offensive on some non-investment level.

Once you pick companies that qualify for your fundamental, conservative standards, you also want to maintain clarity on two other levels: stock ownership and the use of options. Base the decision to hold or sell on consistency in fundamental indicators or on emerging changes in trends. One stock might be a good candidate for option strategies; this does not mean that the stock continues to qualify as part of your conservative portfolio. It makes sense to sell shares of stock as soon as the risk factors change and those factors are clear and precise, based on financial information and capital strength but not on technical aspects of option values.

The second form of clarity is the use of options. A limited number of appropriate strategies are present in your conservative portfolio, and once you have set standards limiting their use, be sure to avoid the temptation to wander from those limited, conservative applications. To review, your criteria may include the following:

1. Use options only for stocks you own or want to own.
2. Use covered calls only if you are willing to accept exercise.
3. Use short puts only if you are willing to buy additional shares, either through a contingent purchase plan or when market movement presents buying opportunities; or plan to close or roll forward to avoid exercise.
4. Premium value from writing short options should be at or greater than a minimum annualized return (e.g., you might use 10 percent as your starting point).
5. Long options should be purchased to (a) protect existing paper profits, (b) exploit unusual and temporary market movements, (c) provide cover for short option positions, and (d) average down your basis in the stock.
6. Long calls may also be used as a form of contingent purchase, but only for stocks you want to buy; it is one way to leverage capital by locking in strike prices on numerous stocks, notably when using LEAPS.
7. Writing short combinations or straddles is appropriate only when the call side is covered and when all possible outcomes have been evaluated and qualified to meet your conservative standards. To

make these short positions more conservative, you can cover short put positions with lower-strike long puts, reducing overall profit but removing market risk.

The Role of Taxes in the Option Equation

Even when you have defined clear guidelines for using options in your portfolio, you may yet face complications due to the tax rules, one of the most troubling aspects of including options as a portfolio strategy. Although everyone hopes for tax simplification, history shows that reforms in the federal tax system have invariably made matters more complex.

A seemingly innocent strategy, such as a short straddle, can cause tax problems. The least of these may be deferral of losses to a future period when a second leg of a straddle closes.

Four Tax Guidelines

A more significant threat than deferral of losses is the removal of long-term capital gains status in exercised stock. Some tax guidelines include:

1. **Limit covered calls to OTM positions.** Using OTM calls avoids the complexities that arise when writing ITM calls.
2. **Accept exposure to loss of long-term capital gains only when you have carryover losses.** If you have large carryover losses, you can maximize options strategies by accepting short-term gains and sheltering them with the carryover loss.
3. **Be aware of how the tax rules affect any combination strategies, especially short straddles.** Be aware of how a specific strategy affects your tax liabilities and rely on your tax advisor to guide you in options taxation matters.
4. **Rolling out of one position and into another could change the status of capital gains taxation.** If you begin with an OTM covered call and then roll forward to a later expiring ITM position, you could trigger the loss of long-term status for the underlying stock.

Option Volatility to Judge Stocks

Tax rules complicate your portfolio. Taxes alone may prevent your entering specific types of transactions. However, knowing the tax outcome in advance provides you with better information and guidelines for proceeding. For most investors, managing market risk—usually measured by degrees of volatility—is a more immediate problem.

The temptation to buy highly volatile stocks specifically to sell covered calls is difficult to resist. But the greatest trap is to start out as a conservative investor and end up with a portfolio of inappropriate stocks. It can happen easily if your selection is based on option-specific valuation rather than on tried-and-true fundamental indicators for selection of the underlying stock. It is not necessary to stray from the conservative standard because it is not difficult to earn options-based returns through conservative strategies.

Volatility as an Early Indicator

Option volatility itself may indicate emerging fundamental problems in a company. The problems may be temporary or permanent. For example, the current quarter's earnings may be lower than expected, which creates momentary volatility. But in the long-term, bigger picture, the company's fundamentals have not changed. In other instances, perhaps a corporation has peaked and is now beginning a gradual downward earnings slide, loss of competitive position, or subtle changes in financial strength. If debt capitalization is inching upward as a percentage of total capitalization, for example, it could signal a change in fundamental strength. This ultimately affects dividends and erodes working capital, recognizing such changes earlier helps you to time decisions. Option volatility is not always an early indicator, but it could be. If option volatility changes suddenly, it is worth the effort to check fundamental trends, evaluate recent news or earnings reports, and look for any confirming signs that the financial strength and position of the company have changed.

Options should be viewed as alternative strategies that may augment the conservative portfolio strategy, provide alternatives to outright purchase, or enable you to protect or take paper profits without having to sell shares.

Option volatility can help you to coordinate your fundamental analysis with technical tests. Degrees of volatility provide potential confirming information or even signal coming changes. In addition to reviewing the fundamentals, technical tests of various types can be used—in conjunction with fundamental analysis—to augment your study of trends. Technical and fundamental volatility are closely related. For example, when a company reports consistent growth in revenues and earnings over time, you are likely to observe a gradual increase in stock market value within a relatively narrow trading range. When the trading range is broader or erratic compared with marketwide trends, it usually signals similar volatility in the fundamentals.

It makes sense to test a limited number of technical indicators along with your fundamentals. These may include option premium volatility as well as trading-range trends and the stock's support and resistance levels. A comparison between fundamental and technical indicators improves your overall program and often provides greater insight than you can achieve with a program limited only to a few fundamental indicators.

The time difference between financial reports and current trends limits the isolated use of fundamentals. Since quarterly and annual reports are outdated by the time they are released, it is difficult to equate these reports to current price trends. However, emerging trends in price volatility provides an indicator of pending financial changes, just as current earnings reports have an immediate effect on the technical side.

It makes sense to consider option volatility within a coordinated fundamental plan; this is especially true if you incorporate technical indicators into your study of a company. Options have no fundamentals of their own since they are derived from the underlying activity, which is why it is so important to limit your use of options to appropriately selected stocks. A conservative portfolio's overall return can be both protected and enhanced with options and done so in a way that remains faithful to your risk profile that is so crucial to your investing success. Avoid the mistake of using options that expose your portfolio to high risk. Isolate your options program to only those strategies that protect your portfolio or that provide premium returns without increasing market risk. As with any range of strategies, the appropriate range of possible uses of options is a short list, and it should be. Inexperienced investors are invariably surprised when they experience losses. Wiser investors know that although some losses are unavoidable, reducing the chances of loss is the key to success. Options can help achieve that while improving overall rates of return in your conservative portfolio.

Class Questions for Discussion and/or Mini-Case Studies

1. Among the pitfalls of using options in a conservative policy is:

    a. a tendency to lose more often than win.

    b. the possibility of a tax audit.

    c. moving away from true conservative decisions.

    d. loss of value in the portfolio because options expire.

2. Allocation by risk profile:

    a. requires that a portion of capital be placed at higher risks than are acceptable.

    b. is essential to protecting capital while earning a good return.

    c. may be the only way to beat the market averages.

    d. should be reserved only for financial professionals.

3. Options can be applied to reduce market risk by:

    a. well-timed covered call trades.

    b. buying puts to protect paper profits and avoid losses.

    c. opening combination strategies that conform to conservative strategies.

    d. all of the above.

Discussion

List the four primary methods for qualifying a company on a fundamental basis and explain how they work together.

Appendix

Option Trading Strategies

Following is a summary of the strategies presented in this book:

1. Basic long call
   a. As a purely speculative position
   b. Used to take advantage of price declines in stock
   c. As a form of contingent purchase

2. Basic long put
   a. As a purely speculative position
   b. Used to take advantage of price rise in stock (insurance for paper profits)
   c. As a form of contingent sale of stock

3. Basic uncovered call
   a. A highly speculative position with unlimited risk
   b. As part of a ratio write

4. Basic uncovered put
   a. As a form of contingent purchase
   b. As part of a rescue strategy

5. Put insurance (buying long puts to ensure current long-stock profits)

6. Contingent purchase strategies
   a. Long calls purchased as an alternative to buying stock
   b. Puts sold to create a credit as well as contingent purchase
   c. The covered long call with higher strike price, shorter expiring short calls

7. Rolling strategies
   a. Rolling forward to defer expiration while creating a credit
   b. Rolling short calls forward and up to defer or avoid expiration and to increase potential exercise price

    c.   Rolling short puts forward and down to defer or avoid expiration and to reduce potential exercise price

    d.   Rolling back—exchanging a current option position for one expiring sooner

8. Ratio write

    a.   Creating partially covered positions with some degree of risk

    b.   Modified to eliminate all risk by buying high calls to offset short exposure

9. Rescue strategies

    a.   Short puts to create a credit and, if exercised, to reduce average basis

    b.   Covered calls to reduce paper loss

    c.   Two-part combination of short puts and, when exercised, converting to covered calls

10. Forced exercise (intentional exercise using covered calls)

11. Spread strategies

    a.   Long spread, high risk requiring adequate price movement

    b.   Short spread with uncovered positions—high risk

    c.   Short spread involving covered call and uncovered put–conservative when fundamental criteria and assumptions are present

12. Straddle strategies

    a.   Long straddle, high risk requiring substantial price movement

    b.   Short straddle with uncovered positions—extremely high risk

    c.   Short straddle combining covered call and uncovered put—ultimate conservative strategy with higher-than-average returns, if fundamental criteria and assumptions are present

13. 1-2-3 iron butterfly

    a.   Low risk with low collateral requirements as long as short and long sides are matched, or long side exceeds number of shorts

    b.   Incomer producing idea, best with strikes one point apart

    c.   High risk if uncovered short side is allowed, requiring collateral equal to 100 percent of strike value; also presents exercise risk when not covered by long side

14. Dividend collar
    a.   Very low risk when strikes are selected above stock basis
    b.   If exercise produces capital gain, no loss occurs
    c.   Eliminates stock market risk while yielding double-digit annualized returns from monthly dividend yield, but only when net option trades create breakeven or credit

Glossary

annualized basis a calculation of return on an option strategy, adjusted to reflect that return as if the position had been open for one year.

at the money (ATM) the status of an option when its strike price is equal to the stock's current market value.

average down a technique for reducing net basis in stock as part of a rescue strategy; by purchasing shares at the current market price, the overall basis in the stock is reduced so that option strategies can be employed to create a net profitable outcome.

call an option providing the buyer with the right, but not the obligation, to purchase 100 shares of a specified stock, at a specified strike price and by an expiration date and obligating a seller to deliver 100 shares at a fixed strike price if the buyer exercises the contract.

closing purchase transaction an order to close a short position through purchase at the current price or premium.

closing sale transaction an order to close a long position through sale at the current price or premium.

combination any strategy involving option contracts on the same underlying stock, when terms (strike price, expiration, or call versus put) are not identical.

core earnings the earnings of a corporation based on inclusion of revenue, costs, and expenses only related to its core business, and excluding all noncore, extraordinary, or other nonrecurring items.

covered call a strategy in which one call is sold for every 100 shares owned; considered a conservative strategy because it reduces market risk while offering exceptional return.

current market value the value of a stock or option based on what a buyer would pay or on what a seller would receive if a transaction was executed now.

deep in or out a condition in which an option is more than 5 points in the money (ITM) or out of the money. A call is ITM when the current market value is higher than the strike price; a put is ITM when current market value is lower than the strike price.

discount a reduction in cost or price, creating a lower basis in stock through selling options.

dividend collar a strategy with a three-part hedge: long stock hedges the short call, the short call pays for the long put, and the long put protects the stock against market price decline; the purpose is to enter into the position, earn the current month's dividend, and then close out through exercise.

dividend yield the yield from dividends paid on stock, calculated by dividing annual dividends by the current value (current yield) of the stock or by the original cost of the stock.

downside protection advantage gained using options to protect long positions through the purchase of an insurance put or through the sale of covered calls.

exercise the purchase of stock under terms of a call, or the sale of stock under terms of a put; exercise takes place at the fixed strike price of the option regardless of the stock's current market value.

expiration the date on which an option becomes worthless.

fundamental volatility the relative tendency of a company's operating results to be consistent from one period to another or to be erratic. The higher the inconsistency of revenue and earnings results, the higher the fundamental volatility.

implied volatility the anticipated future value of an option based on the current market value of the stock and its proximity to strike price, the time remaining until expiration, the stock price volatility, and the transaction volume in the option.

in the money (ITM) the condition in which the stock's current market value is higher than a call's strike price or lower than a put's strike price.

intrinsic value the portion of option premium equal to the number of points, if any, that are in the money (ITM). When the option is at the money (ATM) or out of the money (OTM), there is no intrinsic value.

leverage a strategic utilization of capital to control more capital; for example, a contingent purchase plan involving options is a form of leverage because it locks the purchase price, but the buyer has the right to exercise or not to exercise the option in the future.

listed option an option available to the general public and through public exchanges, which normally expires in 8 months or less.

lock-in price the strike price of an option, which is the purchase or sell price in the event of exercise.

long position a position in a stock or option in which the first transaction is an opening purchase, followed later by a closing sale.

Long-term Equity Anticipation Securities (LEAPS) an option whose life lasts up to 36 months as opposed to a traditional listed option, whose life is limited to 8 months or less.

naked position any short call not covered by an offsetting stock position. A naked call is a short position in which the seller does not own 100 shares of stock for each option written.

opening purchase transaction an order to open a long position through purchase at the current price or premium.

opening sale transaction an order to open a short position through sale at the current price or premium.

option an intangible call or put contract providing certain rights to buyers and obligations to sellers. A buyer pays a premium to acquire rights. The buyer of a call option has the right to purchase 100 shares of stock at a specified strike price and by a specified date in the future. The buyer of a put option has the right to sell 100 shares of stock at a specified strike price and by a specified date in the future. An option seller receives a premium for accepting obligations. A call seller is required to sell 100 shares of stock at a specified strike price and by a specified date in the future if the buyer exercises the call (calls the stock from the seller). A put seller is required to buy 100 shares of stock at a specified strike price and by a specified date in the future if the buyer exercises the put (puts the stock to the seller). In all cases, options exist on a specific stock and cannot be transferred.

out of the money (OTM) a condition in which the current market value of stock is lower than a call's strike price or higher than a put's strike price.

premium the current value of an option, which is paid by the buyer or to the seller for opening a position.

put an option providing the buyer with the right, but not the obligation, to sell 100 shares of a specified stock, at a specified strike price, and by an expiration date and obligating a seller to purchase 100 shares at a fixed strike price if the buyer exercises the contract.

ratio write a variation on the covered call strategy involving the writing of several calls other than one call per 100 shares of stock.

rescue strategy an option strategy designed to offset a net decline in value of stock, using options to average down basis or to offset paper losses with option profits.

return if exercised a calculation of overall return from a short-option strategy, based on exercise of the option and expressed on an annualized basis.

return if unchanged a calculation of return from a short-option strategy, based on expiration of the option and expressed on an annualized basis.

roll down replacement of one short put with another when the strike price of the replacement put is lower than the strike price of the original put.

roll forward a replacement of one short call or put when the strike price remains the same, but the current expiration date is replaced with a later one.

roll forward and up/down a strategy in which an existing option is replaced to avoid exercise, often creating a net credit. An existing short call is closed and replaced with another whose strike price is higher and whose expiration occurs later (roll up); an existing short put is closed and replaced with another whose strike price is lower and whose expiration occurs later (roll down).

roll up a replacement of one short call with another when the strike price of the replacement call is higher than the strike price of the original call.

short position a position in a stock or option in which the first transaction is an opening sale, followed later by a closing purchase.

speculation an investment profile accepting high risk in exchange for the opportunity to earn exceptionally high short-term profits (or to suffer high short-term losses). Speculators are not usually interested in long-term growth or in holding equity positions.

spread a strategy in which options are either purchased or sold on the same stock, with varying strike prices, expiration dates, or both.

straddle a strategy in which an identical number of calls and puts, with identical expiration dates and strike prices, are either purchased (long straddle) or sold (short straddle).

strike price the price at which options are exercised, regardless of the current market value of the underlying stock.

support level the price or price range of a stock representing the lowest likely price that buyers and sellers agree upon.

terms collectively, the contractual conditions and definitions of every option, including identification of the option as either a call or a put, the expiration date, the strike price, and the underlying security.

time value the intangible option premium, equal to all out-of-the-money value and exceeding any intrinsic value.

total return the combined return from option strategies, including option premium, capital gain, and dividend income, all net of transaction costs.

uncovered option a short call when the seller does not own 100 shares of stock for each call written, or any short put.

underlying stock the stock on which an option is bought or sold.

volatility a measurement of safety, the degree of movement in current market value of a stock's price or of an option's premium.

Answers to Questions and Exercise for Discussion

Chapter 1

   1. c

   2. a

   3. b

Discussion: Look for analytical skills of the student. First, did they properly study the key areas of fundamental analysis (dividend yield, dividend increases for 190 years, range of P/E ratio, revenue, net earnings, and long-term debt capitalization). All of these areas should have been studied over a number of years. Second, were students able to make judgments concerning the fundamental strength or weakness of the companies selected?

Chapter 2

   1. c

   2. a

   3. c

Discussion: Study whether students have been able to recognize varying risks based on the moneyness of options. Also look for students' ability to compare risks and opportunities based on premium levels, as well as on time to expiration. This exercise is essential in order to understand how options function and how varying risk levels define a conservative portfolio.

Chapter 3

   1. c

   2. a

   3. c

Discussion: A primary element of timing for covered calls consists of finding a stock chart with current price above the original purchase price. Second, if price has been trending upward but has appeared to plateau, ATM calls are likely to be priced attractively. Selling calls at this top price will be timed well. Look for analytical skill among students in recognizing when current trends are coming to an end and when timing for short trades are ideal.

Chapter 4

1. b
2. a
3. d

Discussion: Look for insights among students into what counts as significant signals and when strong confirmation is also found. Also encourage students to identify patterns of resistance and support, unusual gapping price activity, and other forms of signals beyond reversal.

Chapter 5

1. d
2. a
3. c

Discussion: Students should be able to demonstrate a working knowledge of options to be used in a recovery strategy. With price decline, strategies may involve buying calls to benefit from rising prices; selling puts to benefit from declining time value; or least of all, buying more shares to average down the price. This last method is least desirable because if the price continues to drop, the net paper losses are made worse. With options, the maximum loss is a relatively small premium paid for a call, or the points lost in stock minus the premium received for a short put.

Chapter 6

1. d
2. d
3. c

Discussion: Students should be able to calculate net basis as price per share minus net premium to be received for selling a call. They should also be able to identify the breakeven point for writing a subsequent covered call or uncovered put, as a recovery strategy based on short options.

Chapter 7

1. c
2. b
3. a

Discussion: The 1-2-3 describes the use of three different expiration cycles and a reverse butterfly in the middle area. Look for ability among students to set up an appropriate situation creating a net credit. Also determine whether students have used the proper bid or ask prices, adjusted for trading fee levels. Finally, identify whether students have been able to set up the strategy while avoiding positions expiring in ex-dividend month.

Chapter 8

1. a
2. b
3. b

Discussion: Students should be able to identify the three possible outcomes and calculate the net cost of the position, paper profits in stock, and outcome in each of the three cases. This ability to analytically study the dividend collar is essential to an understanding of the three-part strategy.

Chapter 9

1. a
2. c
3. c

Discussion: Expect students to understand the concept of contingent purchase risk by articulating three methods for reducing both cost and exposure. These should include using higher strikes (for calls) or lower strikes (for puts), both of which will reduce the price of options. However, this also means that reaching a profitable position requires greater price movement than using ATM contracts. A second method is to focus on longer-term options. The greater time to expiration is an advantage, but students should analyze the time benefit versus the higher cost. Third, and perhaps most effective, long-term long calls or puts can be offset by very short-term positions, designed to expire quickly and be replaced, thus eventually paying for the long options.

Chapter 10

1. c
2. a
3. d

Discussion: Students should be familiar with the discussion in this chapter and should explain the following and make accurate comparisons:

margin and collateral requirements, outcome when stock prices rise, out-come when stock prices fall, and dividends.

Chapter 11

1. b

2. a

3. d

Discussion: Look for an understanding not only of the rules, but also how they affect options trading with tax consequences in mind. The wash-sale rule states that a closed position is taxed in the year closed as long as a comparable or identical position is not opened within 30 days. The anti-straddle rule is designed to prevent claiming a net loss this year and profit next year for two-sided transactions. And the unqualified covered call may curtail the ability to claim a favorable long-term capital gain when covered calls are too deep in the money. Students should be able to analyze these rules in the context of planning options strategies to mitigate tax consequences.

Chapter 12

1. b

2. a

3. d

Discussion: The student should be able to explain why the combination of inflation and taxes create the true net breakeven yield investors need. The discussion should include an analysis of how risk and return interact and why it is a mistake to increase risks beyond tolerance levels to meet or exceed breakeven. Look for a clear explanation of the formula $I \div (100 - R) = B$ and what each element of the formula represents.

Chapter 13

1. c

2. a

3. d

Discussion: Expect students to be able to list the four areas: revenue and earnings trends, capitalization and working capital, P/E range over time, and dividend history. Look for a logical analysis of the role each of these fundamental trends plays in defining value of a company and its stock, and also to explain why strong fundamentals translate to safe and strong options positions.

About the Author

Michael C. Thomsett is an expert in technical analysis and stock markets. He has published dozens of books on the topic as well as peer-reviewed papers, magazine articles, and blog entries. He has been writing professionally since 1978 and his best-selling "Getting Started in Options" (John Wiley & Sons) is currently in its 10th edition (published by DeGruyter with a new title, "Options") and has sold over 350,000 copies. The author lives near Nashville, Tennessee and he writes full time.

Index

OTHER TITLES IN OUR FINANCE AND FINANCIAL MANAGEMENT COLLECTION

John Doukas, Old Dominion University, Editor

- *The Art and Science of Financial Modeling* by Anrug Singal
- *Escape from the Central Bank Trap, Second Edition: How to Escape From the $20 Trillion Monetary Expansion Unharmed* by Daniel Lacalle
- *Critical Thinking for Marketers, Volume II: Learn How to Think, Not What to Think* by Terry Grapentine, David Soorholtz, and David Dwight
- *Understanding Cryptocurrencies: The Money of the Future* by Arvind Matharu
- *Understanding Momentum in Investment Technical Analysis: Making Better Predictions Based on Price, Trend Strength, and Speed of Change* by Micheal C. Thomsett
- *Understanding Behavioral BIA$* by Daniel C. Krawczyk, and George H. Baxter

Announcing the Business Expert Press Digital Library

Concise e-books business students need for classroom and research

This book can also be purchased in an e-book collection by your library as

- a one-time purchase,
- that is owned forever,
- allows for simultaneous readers,
- has no restrictions on printing, and
- can be downloaded as PDFs from within the library community.

Our digital library collections are a great solution to beat the rising cost of textbooks. E-books can be loaded into their course management systems or onto students' e-book readers.
The **Business Expert Press** digital libraries are very affordable, with no obligation to buy in future years. For more information, please visit **www.businessexpertpress.com/librarians**. To set up a trial in the United States, please email **sales@businessexpertpress.com**.